Grades 4-8

NotebookReference

Math Fact Book

Second Edition

AMERICAN
EDUCATION
PUBLISHING™

An imprint of Carson-Dellosa Publishing LLC
Greensboro, North Carolina

American Education Publishing™
An imprint of Carson-Dellosa Publishing LLC
P.O. Box 35665
Greensboro, NC 27425 USA

Printed in Minster, OH USA • All rights reserved.   ISBN 0-7696-4340-X

4 5 6 7 8 9 10 11 GLO 15 14 13 12 11 10   10510019763

Table of Contents

Table of Contents

NUMBER SENSE

The History of Roman and Egyptian Numbering Systems

Roman Numerals

Example:

Roman Numeral	Value
I	1
V	5
X	10
L	50
C	100
D	500
M	1,000

Rules for Roman Numerals

◆ When a series of letters goes from a greater to a lesser value, add.
◆ When a series of letters goes from a lesser to a greater value, subtract.
◆ No letter repeats more than 3 times.

VII = 5 + 1 + 1 = 7
CXV = 100 + 10 + 5 = 115
IV = 5 −1 = 4
CD = 500 − 100 = 400
XIV = 10 + (5 − 1) = 10 + 4 = 14
MMCXL = 1,000 + 1,000 + 100 + (50 − 10) = 2,140

STAR GAMES
PART VI

1,000 + 1,000 + 10 + 10 + 1 + 1

62
11
73

2022
2011
11

1,000
1,000
10
10
1
2022

Egyptian Numerals

The **Egyptian** numeral system is based on the number 10. The order of the symbols does not matter. The values of the numerals are added together.

staff	heelbone	scroll	lotus flower	pointing finger	fish	astonished man
(1)	(10)	(100)	(1,000)	(10,000)	(100,000)	(1,000,000)

Example:

 = 23   = 100,100

The Chinese Abacus

The Chinese **Abacus** is the oldest counting machine. The example below shows the number 3,682.

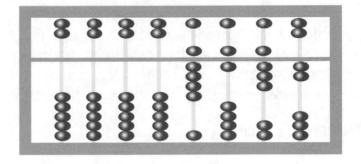

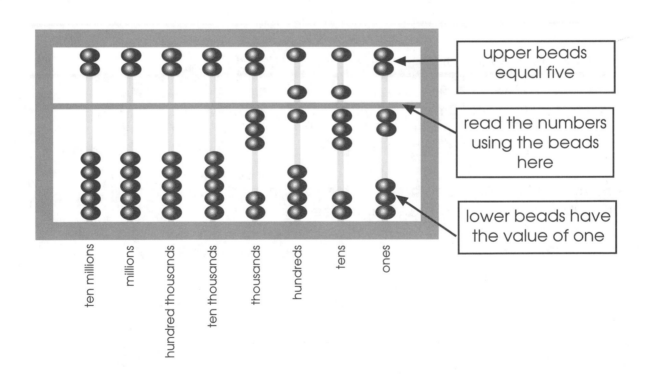

upper beads equal five

read the numbers using the beads here

lower beads have the value of one

ten millions · millions · hundred thousands · ten thousands · thousands · hundreds · tens · ones

Basic Number Concepts

Place value is the position of a digit in a number. A digit's place in a number shows its value. Numbers left of the decimal point represent **whole numbers**. Numbers right of the decimal point represent a part, or fraction, of a whole number. These parts are broken down into tenths, hundredths, thousandths, and so on.

Example:
3,443,221.621

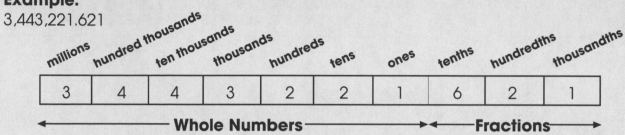

millions	hundred thousands	ten thousands	thousands	hundreds	tens	ones	tenths	hundredths	thousandths
3	4	4	3	2	2	1	6	2	1

←——————— **Whole Numbers** ———————→ ←——— **Fractions** ———→

The chart below shows the place value of each number.

trillions			billions			millions			thousands			ones		
h	t	o	h	t	o	h	t	o	h	t	o	h	t	o
		2	1	4	0	9	0	0	6	8	0	3	5	0

Word form: two trillion, one hundred forty billion, nine hundred million, six hundred eighty thousand, three hundred fifty

Expanded notation is writing out the value of each digit in a number.

Example:
8,920,077 = 8,000,000 + 900,000 + 20,000 + 70 + 7
Word form: Eight million, nine hundred twenty thousand, seventy-seven

Rounding

Rounding a number means to express it to the nearest ten, hundred, thousand, and so on. When rounding a number to the nearest ten, if the number has five or more ones, round up. Round down if the number has four or fewer ones.

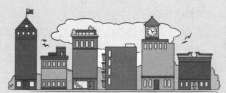

Study how to round a number to the nearest **ten**.

Look at the *ones digit.*

| 46 2 | 46 5 | 46 8 |
| less than 5 | equal to 5 | more than 5 |

Round down to 460.   Round up to 470.   Round up to 470.

Study how to round a number to the nearest **hundred**.

Look at the *tens digit.*

| 82 1 9 | 82 5 9 | 82 7 9 |
| less than 5 | equal to 5 | more than 5 |

Round down to 8200.   Round up to 8300.   Round up to 8300.

Study how to round a number to the nearest **thousand**.

Look at the *hundreds digit.*

| 6 0 35 | 6 5 35 | 6 6 35 |
| less than 5 | equal to 5 | more than 5 |

Round down to 6000.   Round up to 7000.   Round up to 7000.

To **estimate** means to give an approximate rather than an exact answer. Rounding each number first makes it easy to estimate an answer.

Example:

93	90	321	300	1,859	2,000
+ 48	+ 50	+ 597	+ 600	– 997	– 1,000
	140		900		1,000

In an **equation**, the value on the left of the equal sign must equal the value on the right. Remember the order of operations: solve from left to right, multiply or divide numbers before adding or subtracting and do the operation inside parentheses first.

Example: $6 + 4 - 2 = 4 \times 2$

$10 - 2 = 8$

OPERATIONS AND COMPUTATION

Number Operations With Regrouping

Two-Digit Addition With Regrouping

Example:

Steps:

Add the ones.	Regroup, if needed.	Add the tens.
	1	1
78	78	78
+ 43	+ 43	+ 43
	1	121

Three-Digit Addition With Regrouping

Example:

Steps:

Add the ones. Regroup, if needed.	Add the tens. Regroup, if needed.	Add the hundreds.
1	11	11
615	615	615
+ 987	+ 987	+ 987
2	02	1,602

Example:

$$\begin{array}{r} 4,235 \\ -1,917 \\ \hline \end{array}$$

Steps:

Decide if the ones column needs regrouping.
Since 5 is less than 7, regroup.

$$\begin{array}{r} 2 \\ 4,2\cancel{3}15 \\ -1,917 \\ \hline \end{array}$$

Subtract the ones.
The tens column does not need regrouping.
Subtract the tens.

$$\begin{array}{r} 2 \\ 4,2\cancel{3}15 \\ -1,917 \\ \hline 18 \end{array}$$

Regroup the hundreds and subtract.

$$\begin{array}{r} 3\quad 2 \\ \cancel{4},12\cancel{3}15 \\ -1,917 \\ \hline 318 \end{array}$$

Subtract the thousands.

$$\begin{array}{r} 3\quad 2 \\ \cancel{4},12\cancel{3}15 \\ -1,917 \\ \hline 2,318 \end{array}$$

Regroup With Zeros

Example:

Steps:

Subtract the ones.

```
  6, 0 0 5
- 3, 7 3 2
          3
```

Regroup the tens and subtract.
Since there is a zero in the hundreds,
regroup from the thousands.

```
      5  9
  ₅, ₀ 10 5
- 3, 7  3 2
            3
```

Subtract the tens, hundreds, and thousands.

```
      5  9
  ₅, ₀ 10 5
- 3, 7  3 2
  2, 2  7 2
```

You can check your subtraction by using addition.

Example: 34,436   Check: 22,172
            – 12,264   + 12,264
             22,172   34,436

One-Digit Multiplication Without and With Regrouping

One-Digit Multiplication

Here's how to do 1-digit multiplication without regrouping.

Multiply the ones.	Multiply the tens.	Multiply the hundreds and thousands.
2,043 x 2 ——— 6	2,043 x 2 ——— 8 6	2,043 x 2 ——— 4,086

One-Digit Multiplication With Regrouping

Example:

Here's how to do 1-digit multiplication with regrouping.

Multiply the ones. Carry the 5.	Multiply the tens. Add the 5. Carry the 2.	Multiply the hundreds and thousands.
5 4, 1 3 7 x 8 ——— 6	2 5 4, 1 3 7 x 8 ——— 9 6	1 2 5 4, 1 3 7 x 8 ——— 33, 0 9 6

Zero Multiplication and Multiplying by a Two-Digit Number

Zero Multiplication

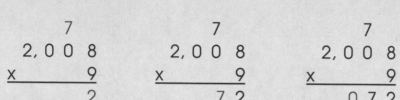

Example:

To multiply with zeros, remember two rules.
1. Zero times any number equals zero.
2. Zero plus any number equals the number.

```
        7                7                7                7
  2, 0 0 8         2, 0 0 8         2, 0 0 8         2, 0 0 8
  x       9        x       9        x       9        x       9
          2              7 2            0 7 2        1 8, 0 7 2
```

Multiplying by a Two-Digit Number

Example:

Multiply each digit by the ones place.	Multiply by the tens place. Place a 0 in the ones column.	Add.

```
   1, 2  2 3          1, 2  2 3           1, 2  2 3
  x      2 3         x      2 3          x      2 3
   3 6 6 9            3 6 6 9             3 6 6 9
                    2 4 4 6 0          + 2 4 4 6 0
                                        2 8, 1 2 9
```

Two-Digit Multiplication With Regrouping and Multiplying by a Three-Digit Number

Two-Digit Multiplication With Regrouping

Example:

Steps:

Multiply by the ones. Carry numbers as needed.	Multiply by the tens. Carry numbers as needed. Put a zero in the ones place.	Add.
5 3 6, 0 7 4 x 3 8 4 8, 5 9 2	2 1 1 6, 0 7 4 x 3 8 4 8, 5 9 2 1 8 2, 2 2 0	6, 0 7 4 x 3 8 4 8, 5 9 2 +1 8 2, 2 2 0 2 3 0, 8 1 2

Multiplying by a Three-Digit Number

Example:

Steps:

Multiply by the ones.	Multiply by the tens. Put a zero in the ones place.	Multiply by the hundreds. Put a zero in the ones and tens place.	Add.
2, 3 1 3 x 1 3 2 4, 6 2 6	2, 3 1 3 x 1 3 2 4, 6 2 6 6 9, 3 9 0	2, 3 1 3 x 1 3 2 4, 6 2 6 6 9, 3 9 0 2 3 1, 3 0 0	2, 3 1 3 x 1 3 2 4, 6 2 6 6 9, 3 9 0 +2 3 1, 3 0 0 3 0 5, 3 1 6

Multiplying by a Three-Digit Number and Properties of Multiplication

Multiplying by a Three-Digit Number With Regrouping

Example:

Steps:

Multiply by the ones. Carry numbers as needed.	Multiply by the tens. Put a zero in the ones place. Carry numbers as needed.	Multiply by the hundreds. Put a zero in the ones and tens places. Carry numbers as needed.	Add.

```
   1 2
   4, 2 0 5
 x   1 7 5
 2 1, 0 2 5
```

```
   1 3
   4, 2 0 5
 x   1 7 5
 2 1, 0 2 5
 2 9 4, 3 5 0
```

```
   4, 2 0 5
 x   1 7 5
 2 1, 0 2 5
 2 9 4, 3 5 0
 4 2 0, 5 0 0
```

```
     4, 2 0 5
   x   1 7 5
   2 1, 0 2 5
   2 9 4, 3 5 0
 + 4 2 0, 5 0 0
   7 3 5, 8 7 5
```

Properties of Multiplication

Example:

Property	Definition	Example
Zero	Any number times 0 equals 0.	$4 \times 0 = 0$
Identity	Any number times 1 equals the number	$4 \times 1 = 4$
Commutative	The order of the factors does not change the product.	$2 \times 3 = 3 \times 2$
Associative	The grouping of the factors does not change the product.	$(2 \times 3) \times 4 = 2 \times (3 \times 4)$

One-Digit Division

Any number can be divided by a 1-digit divisor.

$$1,067 \div 4 \longrightarrow 4\overline{)1,067}$$

Steps:

1. Estimate to place the first digit in the quotient.
2. Multiply the partial product.
3. Subtract. Make sure that the difference is less than the divisor.
4. Carry down the digit from the next place.
5. Repeat for each place.
6. Write the remainder, if necessary.

```
      269R1
  4| 1,077
    - 8↓|
      27|
    - 24↓
      37
    - 36
       1
```

Notice that 4 does not divide into 1. Therefore the first digit in the quotient is in the hundreds, not the thousands, place.

Zeros in the Quotient

Some problems will have a zero in the quotient.

```
      1,026R2
5) 5,132
   −5↓
    01
   −00↓
     13
    −10↓
      32
     −30
       2
```

5 does not divide into 1. Put a zero in the quotient as a placeholder.

Two-Digit Divisors

Steps:

$3,549 \div 23 \longrightarrow 23) \overline{3,549}$

1. Estimate to place the first digit in the quotient.
2. Multiply the partial product.
3. Subtract. Make sure that the difference is less than the divisor.
4. Carry down the digit from the next place.
5. Repeat for each place.
6. Write the remainder, if necessary.

```
      154R7
23) 3,549
   −23↓
    124
   −115↓
     99
    −92
      7
```

Notice that 23 does not divide into 3. Therefore, the first digit in the quotient is in the hundreds, not the thousands, place.

Three-Digit Divisors

Dividing by 3-digit divisors is similar
to dividing by 2-digit divisors.

$6{,}232 \div 164 \longrightarrow 164\overline{)6{,}232}$

Steps:

1. Estimate to place the first digit in the quotient.
2. Multiply the partial product.
3. Subtract. Make sure that the difference is less than the divisor.
4. Carry down the digit from the next place.
5. Repeat for each place.
6. Write the remainder, if necessary.

Example:

```
        38         Notice that 164 does not
164│6,232          divide into 6 or 62. Therefore,
  -492↓            the first digit in the quotient is
   1312            in the tens place.
  -1312
      0
```

```
            25R171
239│6,146
  -478↓
   1366
  -1295
    171
```

Answers in division problems can be checked by multiplying.

Example:

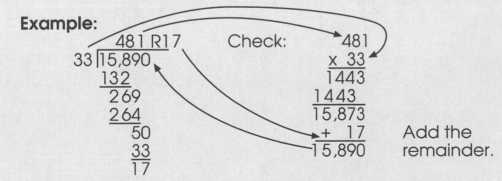

```
      481 R17        Check:        481
33│15,890                          x  33
   132                             1443
   269                             1443
   264                            15,873
    50                           +   17     Add the
    33                           15,890     remainder.
    17
```

Prime and Composite Numbers

A **prime number** is any number greater than 1 that can only be divided evenly by itself and the number 1. The numbers 2, 3, 5, 7, 11, 13, 17, 19, 23, and 29 are the first 10 prime numbers.

A **composite number** is not a prime number. That is, it can be divided evenly by numbers other than itself and 1. The first 10 composite numbers are 4, 6, 8, 9, 10, 12, 14, 15, 16, and 18.

Number Operations With Money

Adding Money

Example:

Steps:

1. Align the decimal points.
2. Add.

$$\begin{array}{r} \$4.32 \\ + \$2.19 \\ \hline \$6.51 \end{array}$$

$$\begin{array}{r} \$10.43 \\ \$\;4.25 \\ + \$12.04 \\ \hline \$26.72 \end{array}$$

Subtracting Money

Example:

Steps:

1. Align the decimal points.
2. Subtract.

$$\begin{array}{r} \$14.32 \\ - \$\;5.43 \\ \hline \$\;8.89 \end{array}$$

Number Operations With Money

Multiplying Money

Example:

Joey buys 14 paperback books for $1.95 each.
How much does he spend?

```
    $1.95
  x    14
     780
  + 1950
   $27.30  ◄──── Set decimal point two numbers in from the right.
```

Dividing Money

Example:

Six friends earn $63.90 shoveling driveways
on a snowy day. If they divide the money
evenly, how much does each one earn?

```
        $10.65
   6 │$63.90
       −6
        3 9
       −3 6
          30
         −30
           0
```

Calculator Basics

A calculator cannot figure out how to solve a problem, but it can make doing computations easier—especially when the numbers are large or difficult. Here are some tips for using one.

1. Estimate answers first to check if the calculated answer makes sense.
2. Enter problems into the calculator twice. It is easy to make a mistake pressing keys.
3. Clear the display before starting a new problem.
4. Hit the = key at the end of each problem.
5. Do not enter commas.
6. Enter numbers in the order you want the calculator to perform the operations. Use the order of operations (**M**y **D**ear **A**unt **S**ally).

Each calculator may be a little different, but all calculators have certain things in common. These keys perform basic operations on almost any calculator.

ON/OFF This key turns the calculator on and off.

AC This key means "all clear." It will clear the display and the memory.

C/CE This key means "clear" or "clear entry." It will clear the display only.

The number keys enter the digits of a number. Enter numbers from left to right. For example, enter 3,840 by pressing **3** **8** **4** **0**

The operation keys add, subtract, multiply, or divide.
+ Add. **-** Subtract. **x** Multiply. **÷** Divide.

The **=** gives the answer after entering all of the operations and numbers.

Here are some examples of how to enter problems into a calculator.

| 3 | 2 | 8 | + | 1 | 9 | 6 | = | **524** |

| 5 | 4 | + | 7 | 8 | + | 3 | 8 | + | 1 | 2 | 3 | = | **293** |

| 9 | 8 | 3 | - | 2 | 3 | 1 | = | **752** |

| 3 | 2 | x | 5 | 4 | = | **1,728** |

| 1 | , | 8 | 9 | 2 | ÷ | 4 | = | **473** |

DECIMALS, FRACTIONS, AND PERCENTS

Decimals

Decimals represent numbers that include a part of a whole. With decimals, the part that is less than 1 is always separated into 10, or a power of 10, parts.

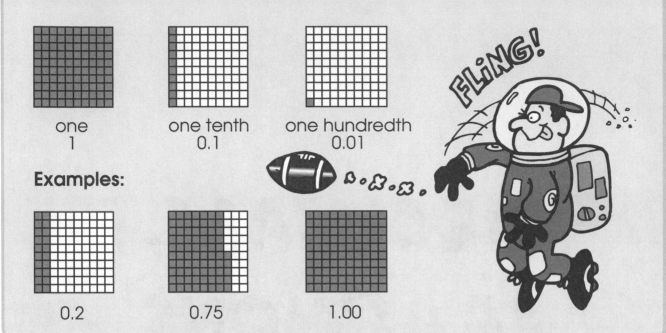

one
1

one tenth
0.1

one hundredth
0.01

Examples:

0.2

0.75

1.00

When writing a decimal, place the decimal point between the ones column and the tenths column. Here are some place values to the right and left of the decimal point.

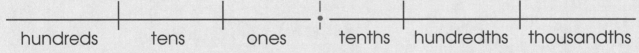

hundreds   tens   ones   tenths   hundredths   thousandths

Steps:
1. Read the whole number.
2. Say the word "and" or "point."
3. Read the number after the decimal point.
4. Say the decimal place of the last digit to the right.

Examples:

45.91 is read "forty-five and ninety-one hundredths"
222.1 is read "two hundred twenty-two point one"
10.004 is read "ten and four thousandths"

Comparing, Ordering, and Rounding Decimals

Comparing and ordering decimals is similar to working with whole numbers.

Example:

Put 6.529, 6.531, and 6.526 in order from greatest to least.

Steps:
1. Align the numbers along the decimal point.　6.529
　　　　　　　　　　　　　　　　　　　　　　　6.531
　　　　　　　　　　　　　　　　　　　　　　　6.526
2. Work from left to right. In this problem, start by comparing the ones place.
3. If all the digits are the same, move to the next place.
4. In the hundredths place, 3 > 2 so 6.531 is the greatest number.
5. In the thousandths place, 9 > 6 so 6.529 is greater than 6.526.
6. 6.531, 6.529, and 6.526 are in order from greatest to least.

Rounding decimals is the same as rounding whole numbers.

Example:

Round 4.386 to the nearest tenth.

Steps:
1. Underline the place to round to and look at the　　4.<u>3</u>86
   digit one place to the right.
2. If this digit is less than 5, the digit you are rounding to stays the same.
   If the digit you are rounding to is greater than or equal to 5, add 1 to
   the place value.

   4.386 is 4.4 rounded to the nearest tenth.

Adding and Subtracting Decimals

Adding Decimals

Adding decimals is a lot like adding whole numbers. Be sure to align the decimal points.

CORRECT

$$\begin{array}{r} 5.349 \\ +\,34.322 \\ \hline 39.671 \end{array}$$

INCORRECT

$$\begin{array}{r} 5.349 \\ +\,34.322 \\ \hline 87.812 \end{array}$$

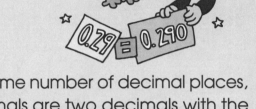

If the numbers being added do not have the same number of decimal places, write an equivalent decimal. Equivalent decimals are two decimals with the same value.

Examples: $0.29 = 0.290$ $1.4 = 1.400$ $3 = 3.000$

Adding zeros to the right of the last decimal digit does not change the value of the number.

Example: $13.83 + 1.264 \longrightarrow \begin{array}{r} 13.830 \\ +\;\; 1.264 \\ \hline 15.094 \end{array}$

Subtracting Decimals

Steps:
1. Align the decimal points.
2. Write an equivalent number if necessary.
3. Subtract as with whole numbers.

Examples:

$15.865 - 3.272 \longrightarrow \begin{array}{r} 15.865 \\ -\;\; 3.272 \\ \hline 12.593 \end{array}$ $3.44 - 0.538 \longrightarrow \begin{array}{r} 3.440 \\ -\,0.538 \\ \hline 2.902 \end{array}$ $2 - 1.894 \longrightarrow \begin{array}{r} 2.000 \\ -\,1.894 \\ \hline 0.106 \end{array}$

Multiplying and Dividing Decimals

Multiplying Decimals

Steps:
1. Ignore the decimal point, and multiply as with whole numbers.
2. Count the number of decimal places in both factors.
3. Place the decimal point that many places from the right in the product.

Example:

$$\begin{array}{r} 0.46 \\ \times\ 0.9 \\ \hline 0.414 \end{array}$$

0.46 ⟶ 2 decimal places
X 0.9 ⟶ 1 decimal place
0.414 ⟶ 3 decimal places

Dividing Decimals

Steps:
1. Move the decimal point in the divisor to the right enough places to make it a whole number.
2. Move the decimal point in the dividend the same number of places to the right. Add zeros if necessary.
3. Divide as with whole numbers.
4. Place the decimal point in the quotient directly above it in the dividend.

Examples:

13.608 ÷ 2.4   0.169 ÷ 0.65   4 ÷ 0.002   1 ÷ 8

$$2.4.\overline{\smash{)}13.6.08}\ \ =\ 5.67 \qquad 0.65.\overline{\smash{)}0.16.90}\ \ =\ 0.26 \qquad 0.002.\overline{\smash{)}4.000.}\ \ =\ 2000 \qquad 8\overline{\smash{)}1.000}\ \ =\ 0.125$$

Fractions and Decimals

Fractions and decimals are two related ways of writing numbers. The amount shaded in these pictures can be shown as a decimal or a fraction.

$\frac{7}{10}$ or 0.7

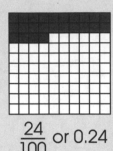

$\frac{24}{100}$ or 0.24

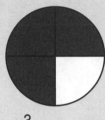

$\frac{3}{4}$ or 0.75

$\frac{1}{2}$ or 0.5

Any fraction can be rewritten as a decimal. To rewrite a fraction as a decimal, divide the denominator into the numerator.

Examples:

$\frac{3}{4}$ → $4\overline{)3.00}^{\,0.75}$ = 0.75

$\frac{9}{20}$ → $20\overline{)9.00}^{\,0.45}$ = 0.45

$\frac{8}{100}$ → $100\overline{)8.00}^{\,0.08}$ = 0.08

$\frac{62}{250}$ → $250\overline{)62.000}^{\,0.248}$ = 0.248

To change a mixed number to a decimal, change the fraction part to a decimal and add it to the whole number.

$4\frac{3}{5} = 4 + \frac{3}{5} = 4 + (3 \div 5) = 4 + 0.6 = 4.6$

$1\frac{7}{8} = 1 + \frac{7}{8} = 1 + (7 \div 8) = 1 + 0.875 = 1.875$

Fractions

Example:

Danny and Mary share a pizza. There are 8 equal slices, and they eat 5. What fraction of the pizza did they eat?

A **fraction** relates the parts of an object or group to the whole. The amount of pizza eaten is:

$\dfrac{5}{8}$ $\longrightarrow$ numerator (the number of pieces eaten)
$\longrightarrow$ denominator (the total number of pieces)

Notice that the object must be divided into equal pieces (slices of pizza) in order to write the fraction. Danny and Mary ate $\frac{5}{8}$ of the pizza, or 5 of the 8 pieces.

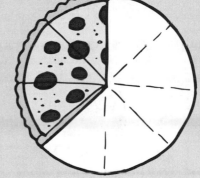

A **mixed number** is the combination of a whole number and a fraction. An **improper fraction** has a numerator larger than the denominator.

Example:

This pictures shows 2 whole squares shaded and $\frac{1}{4}$ of a square shaded. It is shown by the mixed number $2\frac{1}{4}$ or the improper fraction $\frac{9}{4}$.

Steps:

$2\frac{1}{4}$ $\dfrac{2 \times 4 + 1}{4} = \dfrac{9}{4}$ $\dfrac{9}{4} \rightarrow 4\overline{)9}^{\,2R1} = 2\frac{1}{4}$

Writing Decimals as Fractions

To write a decimal as a fraction, write the decimal as a fraction with a denominator of 10, 100, 1,000, or another multiple of ten.

Examples:

0.4 = four tenths = $\frac{4}{10}$

1.29 = one and twenty-nine hundredths = $1\frac{29}{100}$ or $\frac{129}{100}$

0.005 = five thousandths = $\frac{5}{1000}$

4.804 = four and eight hundred four thousandths = $4\frac{804}{1000}$ or $\frac{4804}{1000}$

Factor Trees

A **factor** is a number that can be multiplied by another number to give a certain product. The factors of 24 are 1, 2, 3, 4, 6, 8, 12, and 24 because 1 x 24 = 24, 2 x 12 = 24, 3 x 8 = 24, and 4 x 6 = 24.

Any composite number can be written as the product of prime number factors. The first ten prime numbers are 2, 3, 5, 7, 11, 13, 17, 19, 23, and 29.

FACTOR TREES FOR 24

	24	24	24
	2 x 12	**3** x 8	4 x 6
	2 x 6 x **2**	**3** x **2** x 4	**2** x **2** x **3** x **2**
	2 x **3** x **2** x **2**	**3** x **2** x **2** x **2**	

No matter how a factor tree is made for a given number, the prime factors in the bottom row are always the same.

$24 = 2 \times 2 \times 2 \times 3 = 2^3 \times 3$

To find all the factors of a number, list all the numbers that can divide into it evenly.

3	8	15	24	42	60
1	1	1	1	1	1
3	2	3	2	2	2
	4	5	3	3	3
	8	15	4	6	4
			6	7	5
			8	14	6
			12	21	10
			24	42	12
					15
					20
					30
					60

A number will always have itself and 1 as factors.

Greatest Common Factors (GCF)

Two or more numbers can have **common factors**, or factors that are the same.

24: 1, 2, 3, 4, 6, 8, 12, 24
42: 1, 2, 3, 6, 7, 14, 21, 42

The common factors of 24 and 42 are 1, 2, 3, and 6.

The **greatest common factor** (GCF) is the largest factor shared by both numbers. The GCF of 24 and 42 is 6.

More than 2,000 years ago, the ancient Greek mathematician Euclid invented this handy way of finding the GCF. It is called Euclid's method or Euclid's algorithm.

Example: Find the GCF of 12 and 80.

Steps:

1. Divide the smaller number into the larger one.

$$\overset{6R8}{12\overline{)80}}$$

2. Divide the remainder into the divisor of the first step.

$$\overset{1R4}{8\overline{)12}}$$

3. Repeat until there is no remainder.

$$\overset{2}{4\overline{)8}}$$

4. The divisor in the last step is the GCF.
The GCF of 12 and 80 is 4.

Euclid's method is especially useful when the numbers are very large. A calculator with a remainder function can help compute the division steps.

Example: Find the GCF of 840 and 3,432.

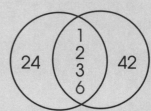

$$\overset{4R72}{840\overline{)3{,}432}} \quad \overset{11R48}{72\overline{)840}} \quad \overset{1R24}{48\overline{)72}} \quad \overset{2}{24\overline{)48}}$$

The GCF of 840 and 3,432 is 24.

Common Multiples

A **multiple** is the product of any given number and a factor such as 1, 2, 3, and so on.

Example:

Multiples of **4**: 4, 8, 12, 16, 20, 24, 28, 32, 36, 40 . . .
Multiples of **10**: 10, 20, 30, 40, 50, 60, 70, 80, 90, 100 . . .
Multiples of **18**: 18, 36, 54, 72, 90, 108, 126, 144, 162, 180 . . .
Multiples of **25**: 25, 50, 75, 100, 125, 150, 175, 200, 225 . . .

Common multiples are multiples that two or more numbers share, or have in common.

Multiples of **8**: 8, 16, 24, 32, 40, 48, 56, 64, 72, 80 . . .
Multiples of **12**: 12, 24, 36, 48, 60, 72, 84 . . .

Some common multiples of 8 and 12 are 24, 48, and 72.

Least Common Multiples and Least Common Denominators

Least Common Multiples

The **least common multiple** (LCM) is the least multiple that a group of numbers has in common. The LCM helps when adding and subtracting fractions.

One way to find the LCM is to find the common multiples and choose the least one.

Multiples of 6: 6, 12, 18, 24, 30, 36, 42, 48, 54 . . .
Multiples of 9: 9, 18, 27, 36, 45, 54, 63, 72 . . .

Common multiples of 6 and 9 include 18, 36, and 54, but the least is 18.

Least Common Denominators

Equivalent fractions make it possible to write any fractions so that they have the same denominator. The **least common denominator** (LCD) is the least multiple that two or more denominators have in common.

Example: Write $\frac{3}{6}$ and $\frac{1}{4}$ with the same denominator.

Steps:

1. Find the least common multiple (LCM) of the denominators. The LCM of 6 and 4 is 12.

2. Rewrite each fraction as an equivalent fraction using the LCD as the denominator.

$$\frac{3}{6} \times \frac{2}{2} = \frac{6}{12} \qquad\qquad \frac{1}{4} \times \frac{3}{3} = \frac{3}{12}$$

The fractions $\frac{6}{12}$ and $\frac{3}{12}$ are the fractions $\frac{3}{6}$ and $\frac{1}{4}$ rewritten with the same denominator.

Fractions

A fraction is in simplest form when the numerator and denominator have no common factors. A fraction that is not in simplest form can be simplified by dividing the numerator and denominator by a common factor.

Examples:

NOT IN SIMPLEST FORM		IN SIMPLEST FORM	
$\frac{2}{4}$	$\frac{21}{48}$	$\frac{1}{2}$	$\frac{7}{16}$
$\frac{30}{40}$	$\frac{9}{15}$	$\frac{3}{4}$	$\frac{3}{5}$

Example: Write $\frac{8}{12}$ in simplest form.

Steps:

1. Find the greatest common factor (GCF) of the numerator and denominator. The GCF of 8 and 12 is 4.
2. Divide the numerator and denominator by the GCF: $\frac{8 \div 4}{12 \div 4} = \frac{2}{3}$

The fraction $\frac{2}{3}$ is $\frac{8}{12}$ written in simplest form.

Adding Fractions and Mixed Numbers

Adding Fractions

Fractions have common denominators if the denominator is the same.

Steps to add fractions with common denominators:

1. Add the numerators.
2. Put the sum over the common denominator.
3. Simplify, if necessary.

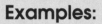

Examples:

$$\frac{1}{8} + \frac{4}{8} = \frac{5}{8} \qquad \frac{1}{6} + \frac{3}{6} = \frac{4}{6} = \frac{2}{3} \qquad \frac{10}{12} + \frac{8}{12} = \frac{18}{12} = 1\frac{6}{12} = 1\frac{1}{2}$$

Adding Mixed Numbers

The steps used to add fractions with common denominators can also be used to add improper or mixed numbers with common denominators.

Examples:

$$\frac{13}{8} + \frac{9}{8} = \frac{22}{8} = 2\frac{6}{8} = 2\frac{3}{4} \qquad\qquad 4\frac{1}{4} + 2\frac{2}{4} = 6\frac{3}{4}$$

$$1\frac{5}{6} + 1\frac{3}{6} = 2\frac{8}{6} = 2 + 1 + \frac{2}{6} = 3\frac{1}{3}$$

Subtracting Fractions and Mixed Numbers

Subtracting Fractions

Steps to subtract fractions and improper fractions with common denominators:

1. Subtract the numerators.
2. Put the difference over the common denominator.
3. Simplify, if necessary.

Examples:

$$\frac{6}{8} - \frac{3}{8} = \frac{3}{8}$$

$$\frac{5}{6} - \frac{1}{6} = \frac{4}{6} = \frac{2}{3}$$

$$\frac{14}{4} - \frac{9}{4} = \frac{5}{4} = 1\frac{1}{4}$$

Subtracting Mixed Numbers

Steps to subtract mixed numbers:

1. Subtract the fractions. "Borrow" from the whole number if necessary.
2. Subtract the whole numbers.
3. Simplify, if necessary.

Examples:

$$\begin{array}{r} 4\frac{3}{5} \\ -2\frac{2}{5} \\ \hline 2\frac{1}{5} \end{array}$$

$$\begin{array}{r} 3\frac{1}{8} \rightarrow 2\frac{9}{8} \\ -1\frac{5}{8} \rightarrow 1\frac{5}{8} \\ \hline 1\frac{4}{8} = 1\frac{1}{2} \end{array}$$

$$\begin{array}{r} 5 \rightarrow 4\frac{3}{3} \\ -4\frac{2}{3} \rightarrow 4\frac{2}{3} \\ \hline \frac{1}{3} \end{array}$$

$$\begin{array}{r} 2\frac{1}{2} \\ -1\frac{1}{2} \\ \hline 1 \end{array}$$

Different Denominators and Subtracting Fractions

Different Denominators

Fractions, improper fractions, and mixed numbers must have a common denominator before they can be added or subtracted.

Steps to add fractions with different denominators:
1. Find a common denominator.
2. Rewrite each number using the common denominator.
3. Add. Simplify, if necessary.

Examples:

$$\frac{3}{8} + \frac{1}{4} = \frac{3}{8} + \frac{2}{8} = \frac{5}{8}$$

$$\frac{5}{6} + \frac{3}{4} = \frac{10}{12} + \frac{9}{12} = \frac{19}{12} = 1\frac{7}{12}$$

$$2\frac{1}{2} + \frac{3}{10} = 2\frac{5}{10} + \frac{3}{10} = 2\frac{8}{10} = 2\frac{4}{5}$$

$$1\frac{2}{3} + 1\frac{2}{5} = 1\frac{10}{15} + 1\frac{6}{15} = 2\frac{16}{15} = 3\frac{1}{15}$$

Fraction Subtraction

Examples:

$$\frac{3}{8} - \frac{1}{4} = \frac{3}{8} - \frac{2}{8} = \frac{1}{8}$$

$$\frac{2}{3} - \frac{2}{5} = \frac{10}{15} - \frac{6}{15} = \frac{4}{15}$$

$$1\frac{1}{6} - \frac{1}{4} = 1\frac{2}{12} - \frac{3}{12} = \frac{14}{12} - \frac{3}{12} = \frac{11}{12}$$

Multiplying and Dividing Fractions

Multiplying Fractions

Example:

Steps:

1. Change mixed numbers to improper fractions.
2. Multiply the numerators. Then, multiply the denominators.
3. Simplify, if necessary.

Examples:

$$\frac{3}{4} \times \frac{1}{2} = \frac{3 \times 1}{4 \times 2} = \frac{3}{8}$$

$$\frac{4}{3} \times \frac{5}{8} = \frac{4 \times 5}{3 \times 8} = \frac{20}{24} = \frac{5}{6}$$

$$2\frac{1}{4} \times \frac{6}{9} = \frac{9}{4} \times \frac{6}{9} = \frac{9 \times 6}{4 \times 9} = \frac{54}{36} = \frac{3}{2} = 1\frac{1}{2}$$

$$\frac{3}{5} \times 10 = \frac{3}{5} \times \frac{10}{1} = \frac{3 \times 10}{5 \times 1} = \frac{30}{5} = 6$$

Dividing Fractions

Write a fraction's reciprocal by switching the numerator and the denominator.

Examples:

The reciprocal of $\frac{3}{4}$ is $\frac{4}{3}$.
The reciprocal of $\frac{5}{2}$ is $\frac{2}{5}$.
The reciprocal of 6 is $\frac{1}{6}$.

Dividing a fraction is the same as multiplying by the reciprocal of the divisor.

Examples:

$$\frac{3}{4} \div \frac{3}{2} = \frac{3}{4} \times \frac{2}{3} = \frac{1}{2}$$

$$\frac{5}{12} \div \frac{5}{8} = \frac{5}{12} \times \frac{8}{5} = \frac{2}{3}$$

$$\frac{40}{7} \div 5 = \frac{40}{7} \times \frac{1}{5} = 1\frac{1}{7}$$

Percents

Understanding Percents

Example:

The word **percent** means "for each hundred."
A test score of 95% means that 95 out of 100
answers are correct.

There are 100 squares in this grid. Each square
represents one hundredth. Since 63 squares
are shaded, 63% is shaded.

Decimals, fractions, and percents are different ways of
representing the same number.

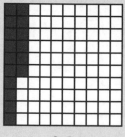

0.16
(sixteen hundredths)

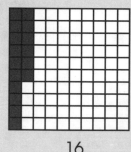

$\frac{16}{100}$

(or $\frac{4}{25}$ in simplest form)

16%

Percents, Decimals, and Fractions

Percents and Decimals

Example:

Steps to change a percent to a decimal, or a decimal to a percent:

PERCENT ⟶ DECIMAL

60% = 60 hundredths = 0.60
3% = 3 hundredths = 0.03
155% = 155 hundredths = 1.55

DECIMAL ⟶ PERCENT

0.35 = 35 hundredths = 35%
0.9 = 90 hundredths = 90%
1.24 = 124 hundredths = 124%

Percents and Fractions

Example:

Steps to change a percent to a fraction, or a fraction to a percent:

PERCENT ⟶ FRACTION

$67\% = 0.67 = \dfrac{67}{100}$

$8\% = 0.08 = \dfrac{8}{100} = \dfrac{2}{25}$

$125\% = 1.25 = \dfrac{125}{100} = \dfrac{5}{4} = 1\dfrac{1}{4}$

FRACTION ⟶ PERCENT

$\dfrac{4}{5} = 4 \div 5 = 0.8 = 80\%$

$\dfrac{1}{3} = 1 \div 3 = 0.333\ldots = 33.3\%$

$1\dfrac{1}{2} = \dfrac{3}{2} = 3 \div 2 = 1.5 = 150\%$

Percent of a Number

Percent of a Number

Example:

Find 30% of 12.

Method 1
Use a fraction.

$$\frac{30}{100} \times 12 = \frac{360}{100} = \frac{36}{10} = \frac{18}{5} = 3\frac{3}{5}$$

Method 2
Use a decimal.

$0.3 \times 12 = 3.6$

30% of 12 is 3   or 3.6.

Figuring Sale Prices

Sale!
All items 20% off

Example:

What is the sale price of the bat?

$34 x 20% = $34 x 0.2 = $6.80
$34 − $6.80 = $27.20

or

100% − 20% = 80%
$34 x 80% = $34 x 0.8 = $27.20

The sale price is $27.20.

RATIOS, PROPORTIONS, AND PROBABILITY

Ratios

A **ratio** is a comparison of two quantities. For example, a wall is 96 in. high; a pencil is 8 in. long. By dividing 8 into 96, you find it would take 12 pencils to equal the height of the wall. The ratio, or comparison, of the wall to the pencil can be written three ways: 1 to 12; 1:12; $\frac{1}{12}$. In this example, the ratio of triangles to circles is 4:6. The ratio of triangles to squares is 4:9. The ratio of circles to squares is 6:9. These ratios will stay the same if we divide both numbers in the ratio by the same number.

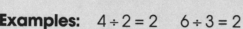

Examples: $\dfrac{4 \div 2 = 2}{6 \div 2 = 3}$ $\dfrac{6 \div 3 = 2}{9 \div 3 = 3}$ (There is no number that will divide into both 4 and 9.)

By reducing 4:6 and 6:9 to their lowest terms, they are the same—2:3. This means that 2:3, 4:6, and 6:9 are all equal ratios. You can also find equal ratios for all three by multiplying both numbers of the ratio by the same number.

Examples: $\dfrac{4 \times 3 = 12}{6 \times 3 = 18}$ $\dfrac{6 \times 5 = 30}{9 \times 5 = 45}$ $\dfrac{4 \times 4 = 16}{9 \times 4 = 36}$

You can find a missing number (*n*) in an equal ratio. First, figure out which number has already been multiplied to get the number you know. (In the first example, 3 is multiplied by 3 to get 9; in the second example, 2 is multiplied by 6 to get 12.) Then multiply the other number in the ratio by the same number (3 and 6 in the examples).

Examples: $\dfrac{3}{4} = \dfrac{9}{n}$ $\dfrac{3}{4} \times \dfrac{3}{3} = \dfrac{9}{12}$ $n = 12$ $\dfrac{1}{2} = \dfrac{n}{12}$ $\dfrac{1}{2} \times \dfrac{6}{6} = \dfrac{6}{12}$ $n = 6$

Proportions

A **proportion** is a statement that two ratios are equal. To make sure ratios are equal, called a proportion, we multiply the cross products.

Examples of proportions: $\dfrac{1}{5} = \dfrac{2}{10}$ $\dfrac{1}{2} \times \dfrac{10}{5} = \dfrac{10}{10}$ $\dfrac{3}{7} = \dfrac{15}{35}$ $\dfrac{3}{7} \times \dfrac{35}{15} = \dfrac{105}{105}$

These two ratios are not a proportion: $\dfrac{4}{3} = \dfrac{5}{6}$ $\dfrac{4}{3} \times \dfrac{6}{5} = \dfrac{24}{15}$

To find a missing number (*n*) in a proportion, multiply the cross products and divide.

Examples:

$$\dfrac{n}{30} = \dfrac{1}{6}$$

$n \times 6 = 1 \times 30$ $n \times 6 = 30$

$n = \dfrac{30}{6}$

$n = 5$

Probability is the ratio of favorable outcomes to possible outcomes in an experiment. You can use probability (P) to figure out how likely something is to happen. For example, six picture cards are turned facedown—3 cards have stars, 2 have triangles, and 1 has a circle. What is the probability of picking the circle? Using the formula below, you have a 1 in 6 probability of picking the circle, a 2 in 6 probability of picking a triangle and a 3 in 6 probability of picking a star.

Example: $P = \dfrac{\text{number of favorable outcomes}}{\text{number of trials}}$ $P = \dfrac{1}{6} = 1:6$

You draw one of the cards shown at the right without looking. You would like to know your *chance* or **probability** of getting a card that says *win*.

Each card (possible result) is called an **outcome**. There are 10 cards. There are 10 possible outcomes. Since you have the same chance of drawing any of the cards, the outcomes are **equally likely**.

win	lose	lose	lose	lose	draw again

draw again	win	draw again	lose

number of outcomes
that say win

number of
possible outcomes

$\dfrac{2}{10}$ or $\dfrac{1}{5}$ Write the probability in simplest form.

The probability of drawing a card that says win is $\dfrac{1}{5}$.

The face of a die have 1,2,3,4,5, and 6 dots.
You roll one die one time.

probability of rolling a 2	probability of rolling a number less than 7	probability of rolling a 7
$\dfrac{1}{6}$	$\dfrac{6}{6}$ or 1	$\dfrac{0}{6}$ or 0

A probability of 1 means the outcome is **certain** to happen.

A probability of 0 means the outcome will **never** happen.

Suppose you flip a penny and a dime. You can show all the possible outcomes in a table or in a tree diagram.

		dime	
		heads	tails
penny	heads	h,h	h,t
	tails	t,h	t,t

A list or a table of all the possible outcomes is called a **sample space**.

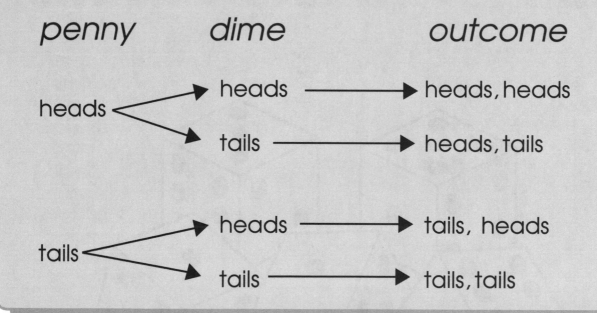

penny	dime	outcome
heads	heads	heads, heads
	tails	heads, tails
tails	heads	tails, heads
	tails	tails, tails

PRE-ALGEBRA

Basic Operations

Addition and multiplication are **commutative operations** because $a + b = b + a$ and $ab = ba$. The numbers can "move about the operation."

Examples: $2 + 3 = 5$ and $3 + 2 = 5$ $2 \times 3 = 6$ and $3 \times 2 = 6$

Note: Subtraction is not commutative because $3 - 2 = 1$ while $2 - 3 = -1$.

For all real numbers, a, b, and c, equality is reflexive, symmetric, and transitive.

Reflexive property: $a = a$
                            Example: $3 = 3$

Symmetric property: If $a = b$, then $b = a$
                            Example: If $6 = 2x$, then $2x = 6$.

Transitive property: If $a = b$ and $b = c$, then $a = c$.
                            Example: If $y = 3x$, and $3x = 12$,
                                           then $y = 12$.

Adding Equations

Letters like a, b, n, x, and so on can be used to stand for numbers.

word phrase	number phrase	
Some number a added to 7	$7 + a$	If $a = 5$, then $7 + a = 7 + 5$ or 12
Some number b decreased by 4	$b - 4$	If $b = 6$, then $b - 4 = 6 - 4$ or 2
The product of 3 and some number n	$3 \times n$ or $3n$	If $n = 2$, then $3n = 3 \times 2$ or 6
15 divided by some number x	$\dfrac{15}{x}$ or $15 \div x$	If $x = 3$, then $15 \div x = 15 \div 3$ or 5

An **equation** like $x + 2 = 9$ states that both $x + 2$ and 9 name the same number.

sentence	equation	
The sum of some number and 2 is 9.	$x + 2 = 9$	$x = 7$ because $7 + 2 = 9$.
Twelve divided by some number is 6.	$12 \div x = 6$ or $\dfrac{12}{x} = 6$	$x = 2$ because $12 \div 2 = 6$.
Seven decreased by some number is 5.	$7 - x = 5$	$x = 2$ because $7 - 2 = 5$.

To solve an equation, you can add the same number to both sides of it.

$$t - 3 = 15$$
$$t - 3 + 3 = 15 + 3$$

$$t + 0 = 18$$
$$t = 18$$

Check
$$t - 3 = 15$$
$$18 - 3 = 15$$
$$15 = 15$$

To change $t - 3$ to t, _____ was added to both sides.

Subtracting, Multiplying, and Dividing Equations

To solve an equation, you can subtract the same number from both sides of it.

$$v + 18 = 47$$
$$v + 18 - 18 = 47 - 18$$
$$v + 0 = 29$$
$$v = 29$$

Check
$$v + 18 = 47$$
$$29 + 18 = 47$$
$$47 = 47$$

To change $v + 18$ to v, _____ was subtracted from both sides.

To solve an equation, you can multiply both sides of it by the same number.

$$\frac{a}{5} = 35$$
$$5 \times \frac{a}{5} = 5 \times 35$$
$$\frac{{}^1\cancel{5} \times a}{\cancel{5}_1} = 175$$
$$a = 175$$

Check
$$\frac{a}{5} = 35$$
$$\frac{175}{5} = 35$$
$$35 = 35$$

To change $\frac{a}{5}$ to a, both sides were multiplied by _____.

To solve an equation, you can divide both sides of it by the same non-zero number.

$$4m = 52$$
$$\frac{4m}{4} = \frac{52}{4}$$
$$\frac{{}^1\cancel{4}m}{\cancel{4}_1} = \frac{\cancel{52}^{13}}{\cancel{4}_1}$$
$$m = 13$$

Check
$$4m = 52$$
$$4 \times 13 = 52$$
$$52 = 52$$

To change $4m$ to m, both sides were divided by _____.

BEYOND BASIC OPERATIONS

Calculating Interest

Interest is the money paid for the use of money.

The amount of interest is determined by:

(1) the **principal,** the amount of money borrowed or deposited,

(2) the **rate** of interest, usually given as a percent, and

(3) the **time**, expressed in years.

When deposited in a savings account, what is the <u>interest</u> on $300 at 5% for <u>1 year</u>?

$$interest = principal \times rate \times time(\text{in years})$$

$$i = 300 \times 0.05 \times 1$$

$$= 15.00 \times 1$$

$$= 15.00 \text{ or } 15$$

$$i = p \times r \times t$$

The interest is $ 15.00

When computing interest for a certain number of days, a year is usually considered to be 360 days. Thus, 90 days is $\frac{90}{360}$ or $\frac{1}{4}$ year, 180 days is $\frac{180}{360}$ or $\frac{1}{2}$ year, and so on.

How much interest would Mrs. Willis pay for a 30-day loan of $600 at 8%?

$$i = 600 \times 0.08 \times \frac{30}{360}$$

$$= 48 \times \frac{1}{12}$$

$$= 4$$

She would pay $ 4.00 interest.

How much interest would Mrs. Willis pay for a 120-day loan of $600 at 8%?

$$i = 600 \times 0.08 \times \frac{120}{360}$$

$$= 48 \times \frac{1}{3}$$

$$= 16$$

She would pay $ 16.00 interest.

Calculating Compound Interest

Interest paid on the original principal and the interest already earned is called **compound interest**.

Bev had $400 in a savings account for 3 years that paid 6% interest compounded annually, What was the total amount in her account at the end of the third year?

At the end of 1 year:

interest = 400 x 0.06 x 1 = 24.00 or $24

new principal = 400 + 24 = 424 or $424

At the end of 2 years:

interest = 424 x 0.06 x 1 = 25.44 or $25.44

new principal = 424 + 25.44 = 449.44 or $449.44

At the end of 3 years:

interest = 449.44 x 0.06 x 1 = 26.9664 or $26.97

Total amount = 449.44 + 26.97 = 476.41 or $476.41

distance = rate x time

$$d = r \times t$$

A robin flew 171 kilometers in 3 hours.
At what speed did the robin fly?

$$
\begin{aligned}
d &= r \times t \\
171 &= r \times 3 \\
\tfrac{171}{3} &= r \\
57 &= r
\end{aligned}
$$

Equation: _____171 = r x 3_____

The robin flew: _____57_____ kilometers

To balance the lever (or scale), how far from the fulcrum must the 12-gram weight be placed?

$$
\begin{aligned}
w \times d &= W \times D \\
10 \times 6 &= 12 \times D \\
\tfrac{60}{12} &= D \\
5 &= D
\end{aligned}
$$

Check

$$
\begin{aligned}
w \times d &= W \times D \\
10 \times 6 &= 12 \times 5 \\
60 &= 60
\end{aligned}
$$

For all levers, $w \times d = W \times D$

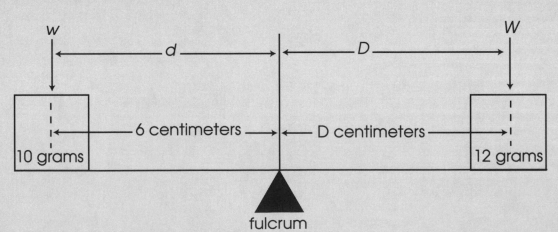

The 12-gram weight must be placed 5 centimeters from the fulcrum.

MEASUREMENT

Customary Units of Length

Standardized units are units that are agreed upon all over the world, so that measurements made in India are the same as measurements made in Iceland, Israel, or Italy. The two main systems are **customary** and **metric**.

Examples:

The customary units for measuring length are **inch (in.)**, **foot (ft.)**, **yard (yd.)**, and **mile (mi.)**.

A paper clip is about 1 inch long.

A notebook is about 1 foot wide.

A baseball bat is about 1 yard long.

A mile is the distance 4 times around a running track.

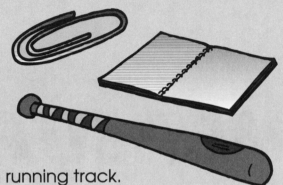

12 inches (in.) = 1 foot (ft.)
3 ft. (36 in.) = 1 yard (yd.)
5,280 ft. (1,760 yds.) = 1 mile (mi.)

To change to a larger unit, divide. To change to a smaller unit, multiply.

Examples:

To change inches to feet, divide by 12.	24 in. = 2 ft.	27 in. = 2 ft. 3 in.
To change feet to inches, multiply by 12.	3 ft. = 36 in.	4 ft = 48 in.
To change inches to yards, divide by 36.	108 in. = 3 yd.	80 in. = 2 yd. 8 in.
To change feet to yards, divide by 3.	12 ft. = 4 yd.	11 ft. = 3 yd. 2 ft.

Sometimes in subtraction you have to borrow units.

Examples:

```
  3 ft.  4 in.  =  2 ft. 16 in.          3 yd.        =  2 yd.  3 ft.
- 1 ft. 11 in.   - 1 ft. 11 in.        - 1 yd.  2 ft.   - 1 yd.  2 ft.
                   1 ft.  5 in.                           1 yd.   1 ft.
```

Customary Units of Weight

Weight measures the force of gravity applied to an object. The customary units for weight are the **ounce (oz.)**, **pound (lb.)**, and **ton (tn.)**.

Examples:

A large strawberry weighs about 1 ounce.

A hardcover book weighs about 1 pound.

A small car weighs about 1 ton.

Here are the main ways to measure weight in customary units:

16 ounces (oz.) = 1 pound (lb.)
2,000 lb. = 1 ton (tn.)
To change ounces to pounds, divide by 16.
To change pounds to ounces, multiply by 16.

As with measurements of length, you may have to borrow units in subtraction.

Example:

	4 lb. 5 oz.	=	3 lb. 21 oz.
	− 2 lb. 10 oz.		− 2 lb. 10 oz.
			1 lb. 11 oz.

BRIDGE
UNSAFE
FOR TRUCKS
OVER
2 TONS

Customary Units of Capacity

Capacity is the measure of how much liquid a container will hold. The customary units of capacity are **fluid ounce** (**fl. oz.**), **cup** (**c.**), **pint** (**pt.**), **quart** (**qt.**), and **gallon** (**gal.**).

Example:

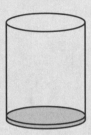 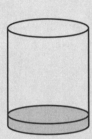  

| 1 c. = 8 oz. | 1 pt. = 2 c. | 1 qt. = 2 pt. | 1 gal. = 4 qt. |

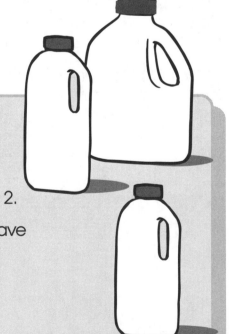

To change ounces to cups, divide by 8.
To change cups to ounces, multiply by 8.
To change cups to pints or quarts, divide by 2.
To change pints to cups or quarts to pints, multiply by 2.

As with measurements of length and weight, you may have to borrow units in subtraction.

Example:
    3 gal. 2 qt. =   2 gal. 6 qt.
    – 1 gal. 3 qt.   – 1 gal. 3 qt.
                     1 gal. 3 qt.

Customary Unit of Temperature

The customary unit of temperature is the degree **Fahrenheit** (**°F**).
A thermometer is used to measure temperature.

Examples:

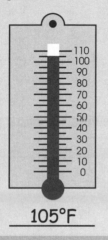

105°F

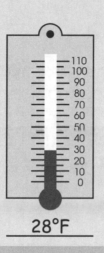

28°F

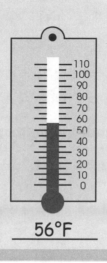

56°F

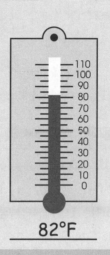

82°F

Example:

Water freezes at 32°F. It boils at 212°F.

30°F is cold   70°F is warm
50°F is cool   90°F is hot

The Metric System

The **metric system** is another standardized system of measurement. It is based on the number 10, which makes it easy to understand and use. This chart shows the basic units.

Measurement	Basic Unit
length	meter
weight	gram
capacity	liter

Prefixes are added to the names of basic units to form greater and lesser units. This chart lists some prefixes. The common ones are shown in bold.

Prefix	Relation to the basic unit as a fraction	As a decimal
Milli - (m)	1/1,000	0.001
Centi - (c)	1/100	0.01
Deci - (d)	1/10	0.1
Basic units	1	
Deka - (da)	10	
Hecto - (h)	100	
Kilo - (k)	1,000	

Length is measured in meters (m).
1 kilometer (km) = 1,000 meters
1 centimeter (cm) = 0.01 meters
1 millimeter (mm) = 0.001 meters

Weight is measured in grams (g).
1 kilogram (kg) = 1,000 grams
1 centigram (cg) = 0.01 grams
1 milligram (mg) = 0.001 grams

Capacity is measured in liters (L).
1 kiloliter (kL) = 1,000 liters
1 centiliter (cL) = 0.01 liters
1 milliliter (mL) = 0.001 liters

Metric Units of Length

The basic metric unit of length is the **meter**. The most common units are the **millimeter (mm)**, **centimeter (cm)**, **meter (m)**, and **kilometer (km)**.

This line is 1 millimeter long.   -

This line is about 1 centimeter long.   —

A baseball bat is about 1 meter long.

A kilometer is about the distance
2 times around a running track.

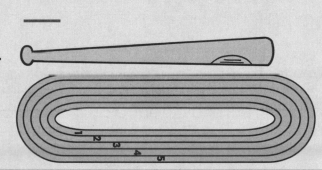

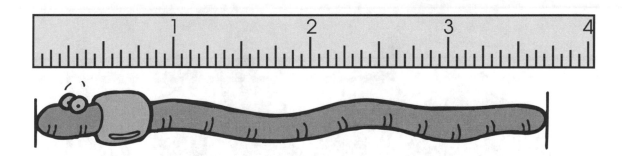

A **meter (m)** is about 40 inches or 3.3 feet.
A **centimeter (cm)** is $\frac{1}{100}$ of a meter or 0.4 inches.
A **millimeter (mm)** is $\frac{1}{1000}$ of a meter or 0.04 inches.
A **kilometer (km)** is 1,000 meters or 0.6 miles.

As before, divide to find a larger unit and multiply to find a smaller unit.

Examples:
    To change cm to mm, multiply by 10.
    To change cm to meters, divide by 100.
    To change mm to meters, divide by 1,000.
    To change km to meters, multiply by 1,000.

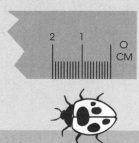

Metric Units of Capacity

The basic metric unit of capacity is the **liter**. The most common units are the **milliliter (ml)** and **liter (L)**.

Example:

A soda cap holds about 1 milliliter.
One liter is a little larger than a quart.

Steps to calculate how close you estimated:
1. Subtract the lesser number from the greater.
2. Divide the difference by the actual capacity.
3. Multiply by 100 to get a percentage. Round to the ones, if necessary.

A **liter (L)** is a little over 1 quart.
A **milliliter (mL)** is $\frac{1}{1000}$ of a liter or about 0.03 oz.
A **kiloliter (kL)** is 1,000 liters or about 250 gallons.

Metric Units of Weight

The basic metric unit of weight is the **gram**. The most common units are the **milligram (mg)**, **gram (g)**, and **kilogram (kg)**.

Example:

A short human hair weighs about 1 milligram.

A paper clip weighs about 1 gram.

A textbook weighs about 1 kilogram.

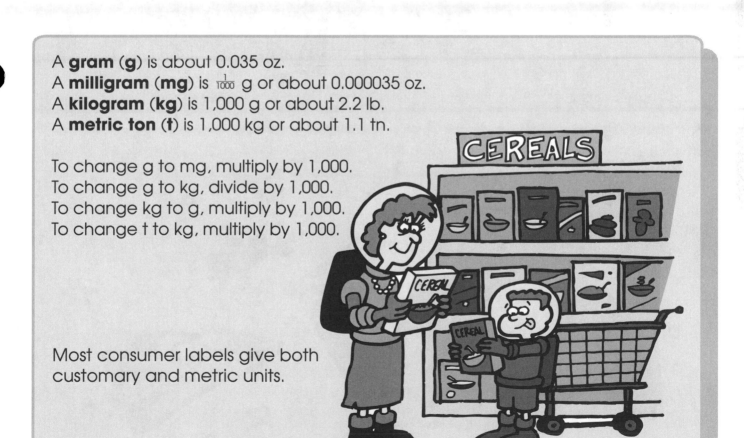

A **gram (g)** is about 0.035 oz.
A **milligram (mg)** is $\frac{1}{1000}$ g or about 0.000035 oz.
A **kilogram (kg)** is 1,000 g or about 2.2 lb.
A **metric ton (t)** is 1,000 kg or about 1.1 tn.

To change g to mg, multiply by 1,000.
To change g to kg, divide by 1,000.
To change kg to g, multiply by 1,000.
To change t to kg, multiply by 1,000.

Most consumer labels give both customary and metric units.

Metric Units of Volume

In the metric system, the units for length and capacity are related.

Example:

A milliliter is equivalent to a cube that measures 1 centimeter on each side (called a cubic centimeter or cm³).

Since a liter is 1,000 milliliters, a liter equals 1,000 cubic centimeters.

1 milliliter

1 cm
1 cm
1 cm

1 cm
1 cm
1 cm

10 cm
10 cm
10 cm

Metric Unit of Temperature

The metric unit of temperature is the degree **Celsius** (°**C**). A thermometer is used to measure temperature.

Examples:

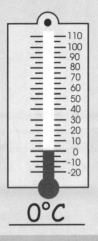

0°C

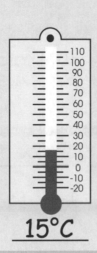

15°C

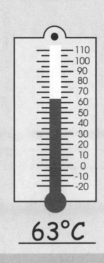

63°C

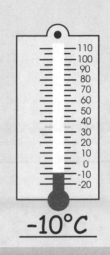

−10°C

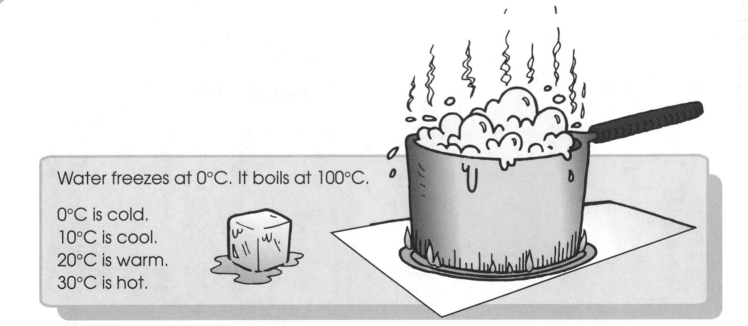

Water freezes at 0°C. It boils at 100°C.

0°C is cold.
10°C is cool.
20°C is warm.
30°C is hot.

Customary to Metric and Metric to Customary Conversions

Length Conversion

Customary lengths can be converted to metric, and vice versa, using these facts. Some measurements are not exact and have the approximate symbol (≈) instead of the equal sign.

1 inch = 2.54 centimeters   1 centimeter ≈ 0.3937 inch
1 yard = 0.9144 meters   1 meter ≈ 1.094 yards
1 mile ≈ 1.609 kilometers   1 kilometer ≈ 0.621 miles

Examples:

6 inches = _____ centimeters
6 x 2.54 centimeters = 15.24 centimeters

44 kilometers = _____ miles
44 x .621 miles = 27.324 miles

Weight Conversion

1 ounce ≈ 28.35 grams   1 gram ≈ 0.035 ounce
1 pound ≈ 0.454 kilograms   1 kilogram ≈ 2.2 pounds

Examples:

4 ounces = _____ grams
4 x 28.35 grams = 113.4 grams

1.6 kilograms = _____ pounds
1.6 x 2.2 pounds = 3.52 pounds

Customary to Metric and Metric to Customary Conversions

1 fluid ounce ≈ 29.57 milliliters   1 milliliter ≈ 0.034 fluid ounce
1 quart ≈ 0.946 liters   1 liter ≈ 1.057 quarts

Examples:

65 milliliters = _____ fluid ounces
65 x 0.034 fluid ounces = 2.21 fluid ounces

5 quarts = _____ liters
5 x 1.057 liters = 4.73 liters

This equation shows how Celsius and Fahrenheit are related.

$°F = 1.8 \times °C + 32$

Examples:

Steps to find the Fahrenheit temperature, given a Celsius temperature:
1. Multiply by 1.8.
2. Add 32°.

15°C = _____ °F
(15 x 1.8) + 32 = 27 + 32 = 59°F

Steps to find Celsius temperature, given a Fahrenheit temperature:
1. Subtract 32.
2. Divide by 1.8.

50°F = _____ °C
(50 – 32) ÷ 1.8 = 18 ÷ 1.8 = 10°C

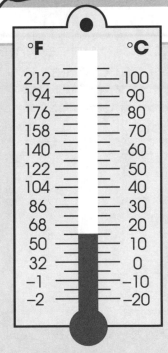

Conversion Chart

Linear Measure

To convert:	Multiply by:	To convert:	Multiply by:
inches to millimeters	25.4	millimeters to inches	0.039
inches to centimeters	2.54	centimeters to inches	0.394
feet to meters	0.305	meters to feet	3.281
yards to meters	0.914	meter to yards	1.094
miles to kilometers	1.609	kilometers to miles	0.621

Square Measure

To convert:	Multiply by:	To convert:	Multiply by:
sq. inches to sq. centimeters	6.452	sq. centimeters to sq. inches	0.155
sq. feet to sq. meters	0.093	sq. meters to sq. feet	10.764
sq. yards to sq. meters	0.836	sq. meters to sq. yards	1.196
acres to hectares	0.405	hectares to acres	2.471

Cubic Measure

To convert:	Multiply by:	To convert:	Multiply by:
cu. inches to cu. centimeters	16.387	cu. centimeters to cu. inches	0.061
cu. feet to cu. meters	0.028	cu. meters to cu. feet	35.315
cu. yards to cu. meters	0.765	cu. meters to cu. yards	1.308

Conversion Chart

Liquid Measure

To convert:	Multiply by:	To convert:	Multiply by:
fluid ounces to liters	0.03	liters to fluid ounces	33.814
quarts to liters	0.946	liters to quarts	1.057
gallons to liters	3.785	liters to gallons	0.264
imperial gallons to liters	4.546	liters to imperial gallons	0.220

Weights

To convert:	Multiply by:	To convert:	Multiply by:
ounces avoirdupois to grams	28.35	grams to ounces avoirdupois	0.035
pounds avoirdupois to kilograms	0.454	kilograms to pounds avoirdupois	2.205
tons to metric tons	0.907	metric tons to tons	1.102

Temperature

	Fahrenheit	Celsius
Freezing point of water	32° F	0° C
Boiling point of water	212° F	100° C
Body temperature	98.6° F	37° C

- To find degrees Celsius, subtract 32 from degrees Fahrenheit and divide by 1.8
  Example: 68° F = (68 − 32)/1.8 = 20° C

- To find degrees Fahrenheit, multiply degrees Celsius by 1.8 and add 32
  Example: 35° C = (35 x 1.8) + 32 = 95° F

Measuring Time

Another type of measurement is **time**. This is not measured in customary and metric units. It is universal.

The standard units of time are the **second (sec.)**, **minute (min.)**, **hour (hr.)**, and **day (d.)**.

Example:

It takes about 1 second to snap your fingers.
It takes about 1 minute to get dressed.
A television drama usually lasts 1 hour.

Adding and Subtracting Time

Examples:

```
   4 hours   32 minutes
+ 2 hours   29 minutes
   6 hours   61 minutes = 7 hours 1 minute
```

```
   7 hours   12 minutes = 6 hours 72 minutes
− 5 hours   28 minutes = 5 hours 28 minutes
                         1 hour  44 minutes
```

Example:

1 minute = 60 seconds
1 hour = 60 minutes = 3,600 seconds
1 day = 24 hours = 1,400 minutes = 86,400 seconds

4 days x 24 hours = 4 x 24 hours = 96 hours

In most cases, this is how to change time through different time zones: Subtract one hour for each time zone traveled to the west. Add one hour when traveling east.

Sample Times

Hawaii Time: 2:00 a.m.

Alaska Time: 3:00 a.m.

Pacific Time: 4:00 a.m.

Mountain Time: 5:00 a.m.

Central Time: 6:00 a.m.

Eastern Time: 7:00 a.m.

Atlantic Time: 8:00 a.m.

Newfoundland Time: 8:30 a.m.

Greenland Time: 9:00 a.m.

Example: What time is it in Seattle, when it is 3:15 P.M. in Chicago?

Seattle is 2 time zones west of Chicago. Subtract 2 hours. The time is 1:15 P.M.

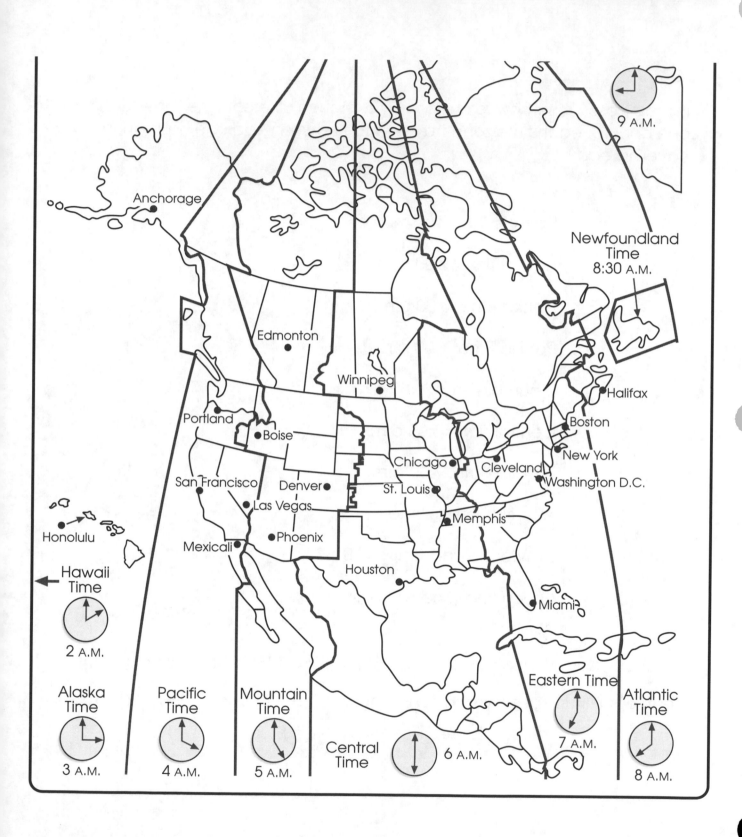

Anchorage

Newfoundland
Time
8:30 A.M.

9 A.M.

Edmonton

Winnipeg

Halifax

Portland

Boise

Chicago

Cleveland

New York

Boston

San Francisco

Denver

St. Louis

Washington D.C.

Las Vegas

Memphis

Honolulu

Mexicali

Phoenix

Houston

Hawaii
Time

Miami

2 A.M.

Alaska
Time

Pacific
Time

Mountain
Time

Eastern Time

Atlantic
Time

Central
Time

7 A.M.

3 A.M.

4 A.M.

5 A.M.

6 A.M.

8 A.M.

PROBLEM SOLVING

Methods of Problem Solving

Trial and Error

Often, the quickest way to solve a problem is to make a logical guess and test it to see if it works. The first guess, or trial, will probably not be the correct answer—but it should help figure out a better, more reasonable guess.

Choosing a Method

This table explains different methods of computation that can be used to solve a problem.

Method		
Mental Math	– Calculating in your head.	– Use with small numbers, memorized facts, and multiples of tens, hundreds, thousands, and so on.
Objects/Diagram	– Drawing or using an object to represent the problem.	– Use to model the situation.
Pencil and Paper	– Calculating the answer on paper.	– Use when a calculator is not available and the problem is too difficult to solve mentally.
Calculator	– Using a calculator or computer to find the solution.	– Use with large numbers or for a quick answer.
Trial and Error	– Making a guess at the answer and trying to see if it works.	– Use when unsure what to do or if none of the methods above work.

Choosing the Operation

Before solving a word problem, choose which operation to use—addition, subtraction, multiplication, division, or a combination. The context of the problem is the most important clue to help choose, but there are certain clue words that may help you decide.

Addition	Subtraction	Multiplication	Division
in all	less	join	divide
sum	less than	combine	separate
total	minus	twice	split
altogether	how much more/less	triple	how many groups
more than	difference	times more	
combined	decrease		
	compare		

Example: Rasheed has 4 more books than Tommy. Tommy has 7 books. How many does Rasheed have?

Solution: Since Rasheed has more books, add. 7 + 4 = 11. Rasheed has 11 books.

"Be careful! Clue words can be misleading so always understand what a problem is asking for before solving it."

Finding a Pattern and Drawing a Picture

Find a Pattern

Finding a pattern can help solve a problem. To use this strategy, look for a way to describe the relationships, then use the pattern to solve the problem.

Example: Find the missing number and state the pattern.

256   128   64   _____   16   8

The rule is to divide each number by 2 to get the next number. The missing number is 32.

Draw a Picture

Many problems can be solved more easily by drawing a picture. The picture could be a diagram, list, chart, graph, or table.

Clues that you might draw a picture:

1. The problem is about geometry or a physical object.
2. You want to visualize what is happening.

Example: How many triangles are created when you draw the diagonals of a square?

1. Draw the square.
2. Draw the diagonals.
3. Count the triangles.

There are 8 triangles.

Example: A sandwich shop offers tuna, turkey, and ham. These meats can be served on white or wheat bread. How many different sandwiches can they make?

There are 6 different kinds of sandwiches.

tuna	white
tuna	wheat
turkey	white
turkey	wheat
ham	white
ham	wheat

Working Backwards

Usually a problem is solved by working from the beginning to the end. Sometimes you can "work backwards" from the end to the beginning to solve problems.

Example: On a trip to the amusement park, the Millers spend $98. Food costs $25 and parking costs $13. How much was the price of admission (assume there are no other costs)?

98	− 25	− 13	= 60
total cost	subtract the other costs that were originally added to the total		admission

The admission costs are $60.

Example: Brandon brought some cookies to school. He gave 6 to the teacher and divided the rest into 21 groups of 2 each for the students. How many cookies did he bring?

2 x 21	+ 6	= 48
multiply to "undo" the division of the cookies	add to "undo" the cookies given away	total number

Brandon brought 48 cookies.

Clues that you might work backwards:

1. The final result of a problem is given but the original parts are not.
2. The problem includes a series of steps that can be reversed—such as division can be reversed by multiplication.
3. The problem is complicated at the beginning and simpler at the end.

Other Methods of Solving Problems

Multi-Step Problems

Some problems take more than one step to solve. First, plan each step needed to find the solution. Then solve each part to find the answer.

Example: Tickets for a bargain matinee cost $4 for adults and $3 for children. How much would tickets cost for a family of 2 adults and 3 children?

Step 1: Find the cost of the adults' tickets.

Step 2: Find the cost of the children's tickets.

Step 3: Add to find the sum of the tickets.

2 adults	x	$4 each ticket	=	$8 total
3 children	x	$3 each ticket	=	$9 total
$8 adults	+	$9 children	=	$17 total

The tickets cost $17 total.

Hidden Questions

When solving a story problem, you may find that some information you want is not stated in the problem. You must ask yourself what information you need and decide how you can use the data in the problem to find this information. The problem contains a hidden question to find before you can solve it.

Example: Chris and his mother are building a birdhouse. He buys 4 pieces of wood for $2.20 each. How much change should he get back from $10?

Step 1: Find the hidden question:
What is the total cost of the wood?

$2.20 \times 4 = $8.80

Step 2: Use your answer to the hidden question to solve the problem.

$10.00 - $8.80 = $1.20

GEOMETRY

Points, Lines, and Rays

Geometry is the branch of mathematics that has to do with points, lines, and shapes.

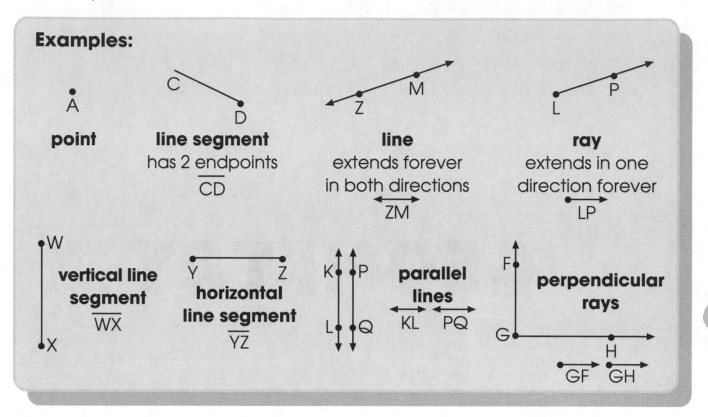

Examples:

• A

point

C
D

line segment
has 2 endpoints
$\overline{CD}$

Z M

line
extends forever
in both directions
$\overleftrightarrow{ZM}$

L P

ray
extends in one
direction forever
$\overrightarrow{LP}$

•W
•X

**vertical line
segment**
$\overline{WX}$

Y Z

**horizontal
line segment**
$\overline{YZ}$

K P
L Q

**parallel
lines**
$\overleftrightarrow{KL}$ $\overleftrightarrow{PQ}$

F
G H

**perpendicular
rays**
$\overrightarrow{GF}$ $\overrightarrow{GH}$

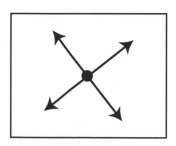

Intersecting lines
meet at a point.

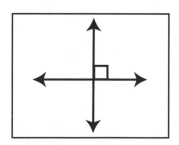

Perpendicular lines
intersect and form
a right angle.

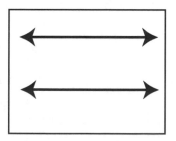

Parallel lines are
in the same plane
and never intersect.

Types of Angles

When two line segments come together, they form an angle.

angle BAC
∠ BAC
∠ A

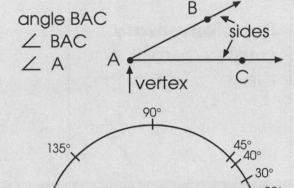

Angles are measured in units called degrees (°). A half-circle has 180°. Angles can be measured with a protractor.

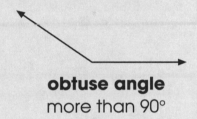

The number of degrees in an angle determines what kind of angle it is.

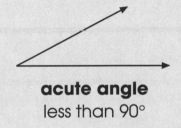

acute angle
less than 90°

obtuse angle
more than 90°

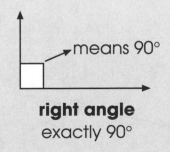

means 90°

right angle
exactly 90°

A **straight angle** equals exactly 180°.

Supplementary angles combine to make a 180° angle.

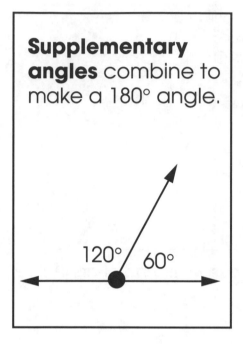

Complementary angles combine to make a 90° angle.

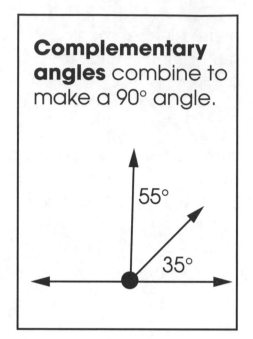

Adjacent angles share a vertex and a ray.

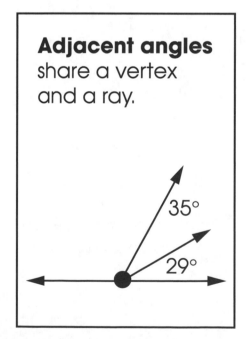

Vertical angles are not adjacent, but they share a vertex and are congruent.

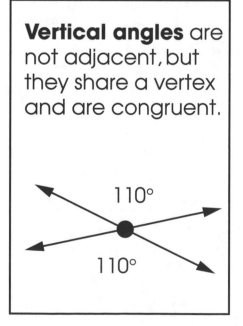

Polygons

The word **polygon** means "many angles" and describes a shape that:

a) starts and stops at the same place (making it "closed").
b) can be traced without lifting the pencil or crossing or retracing any part.
c) is made of at least three line segments.

Polygons are classified by the number of sides they have and by the lengths of their sides.

3 sides—triangle	7 sides—heptagon
4 sides—quadrilateral	8 sides—octagon
5 sides—pentagon	9 sides—nonagon
6 sides—hexagon	10 sides—decagon

A **regular polygon** has sides that are all the same length.

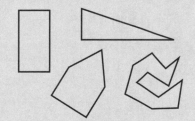

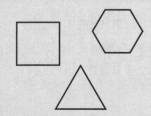

shapes   **polygons**   **regular polygons**

Triangles

A **triangle** is a three-sided polygon. It has three sides and three angles.

Triangles can be classified by the lengths of their sides.

scalene
zero sides
of equal length

isosceles
two sides
of equal length

equilateral
three sides
of equal length

Triangles can also be classified by the kinds of angles they have.

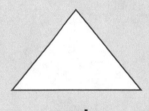

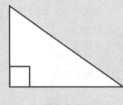

acute
all three angles
less than 90°

right
one angle is
exactly 90°

obtuse
one angle is more
than 90°

The sum of the three angles in a triangle always adds up to 180°.

Examples:

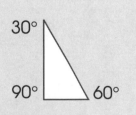

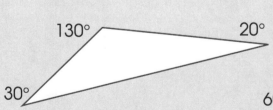

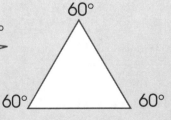

90° + 30° + 60° = 180°   130° + 30° + 20° = 180°   60° + 60° + 60° = 180°

Quadrilaterals

A **quadrilateral** is a shape with four sides and four angles. The sum of angles in all quadrilaterals is 360°. Like triangles, quadrilaterals come in different shapes and are categorized by their sides and their angles.

A **square** has four parallel sides of equal length and four 90° angles.

A **rectangle** has four parallel sides, but only its opposite sides are equal length; it has four 90° angles.

A **parallelogram** has four parallel sides, with the opposite sides of equal length, but all its angles are more than or less than 90°.

A **trapezoid** has two opposite sides that are parallel; its sides may or may not be equal length; its angles may include none, one or two that are 90°.

Circles

A **circle** is a shape on which all of the points on it are the same distance from a given point. This diagram shows the parts of circle K.

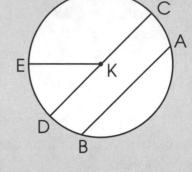

center
K
the point from which all points on a circle are the same distance

diameter
CD
a line segment that connects two points on a circle and passes through the center

radius
EK
a line segment that connects the center with any point on the circle
The plural of radius is radii.

chord
AB
a line segment that connects two points on a circle but does not pass through the center point

A geometric shape that can be separated into two identical parts is **symmetric**. If the shape is folded along the line of symmetry, the two halves will match.

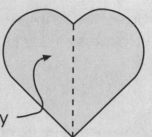

line of symmetry

A **line of symmetry** divides a shape into two matching halves. A shape can have any number of lines of symmetry.

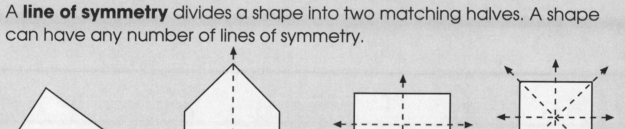

| 0 lines of symmetry | 1 line of symmetry | 2 lines of symmetry | 4 lines of symmetry |

Alphabet Symmetry

The letter B has a horizontal line of symmetry
The letter W has a vertical line of symmetry

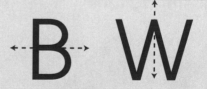

Congruent and Similar Shapes

Shapes are **congruent** if they are exactly the same size and shape.

congruent

Shapes are **similar** if they are about the same relative size.

similar

You can slide, flip, and rotate shapes. These changes are called **transformations**.

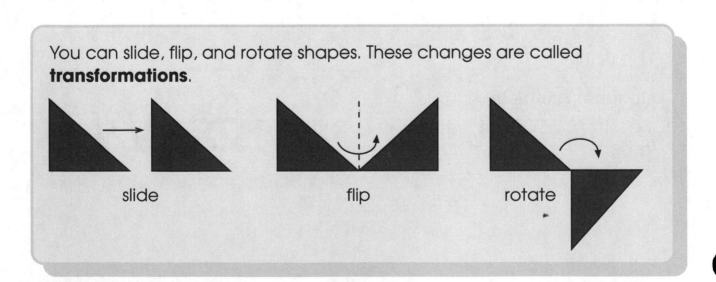

slide   flip   rotate

Square Roots

Study how the table is used to find the square and the square root of a number *n*. (≈ is read *is approximately equal to.*)

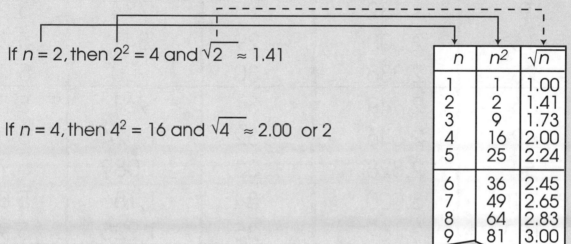

If *n* = 2, then 2^2 = 4 and $\sqrt{2}$ ≈ 1.41

If *n* = 4, then 4^2 = 16 and $\sqrt{4}$ ≈ 2.00 or 2

n	n^2	$\sqrt{n}$
1	1	1.00
2	2	1.41
3	9	1.73
4	16	2.00
5	25	2.24
6	36	2.45
7	49	2.65
8	64	2.83
9	81	3.00

Table of Squares and Square Roots

n	n²	√n	n	n²	√n
1	1	1.000	26	676	5.099
2	4	1.414	27	729	5.196
3	9	1.732	28	784	5.292
4	16	2.000	29	841	5.385
5	25	2.236	30	900	5.477
6	36	2.449	31	961	5.568
7	49	2.646	32	1,024	5.657
8	64	2.828	33	1,089	5.745
9	81	3.000	34	1,156	5.831
10	100	3.162	35	1,225	5.916
11	121	3.317	36	1,296	6.000
12	144	3.464	37	1,369	6.083
13	169	3.606	38	1,444	6.164
14	196	3.742	39	1,521	6.245
15	225	3.873	40	1,600	6.325
16	256	4.000	41	1,681	6.403
17	289	4.123	42	1,764	6.481
18	324	4.243	43	1,849	6.557
19	361	4.359	44	1,936	6.633
20	400	4.472	45	2,025	6.708
21	441	4.583	46	2,116	6.782
22	484	4.690	47	2,209	6.856
23	529	4.796	48	2,304	6.928
24	576	4.899	49	2,401	7.000
25	625	5.000	50	2,500	7.071

Table of Squares and Square Roots

n	n^2	$\sqrt{n}$	n	n^2	$\sqrt{n}$
51	2,601	7.141	76	5,776	8.718
52	2,704	7.211	77	5,929	8.775
53	2,809	7.280	78	6,084	8.832
54	2,916	7.348	79	6,241	8.888
55	3,025	7.416	80	6,400	8.944
56	3,136	7.483	81	6,561	9.000
57	3,249	7.550	82	6,724	9.055
58	3,364	7.616	83	6,889	9.110
59	3,481	7.681	84	7,056	9.165
60	3,600	7.746	85	7,225	9.220
61	3,721	7.810	86	7,396	9.274
62	3,844	7.874	87	7,569	9.327
63	3,969	7.937	88	7,744	9.381
64	4,096	8.000	89	7,921	9.434
65	4,225	8.062	90	8,100	9.487
66	4,356	8.124	91	8,281	9.539
67	4,489	8.185	92	8,464	9.592
68	4,624	8.246	93	8,649	9.644
69	4,761	8.307	94	8,836	9.695
70	4,900	8.367	95	9,025	9.747
71	5,041	8.426	96	9,216	9.798
72	5,184	8.485	97	9,409	9.849
73	5,329	8.544	98	9,604	9.899
74	5,476	8.602	99	9,801	9.950
75	5,625	8.660	100	10,000	10.000

Study how the table on the previous page can be used to find the square root of a number greater than 150.

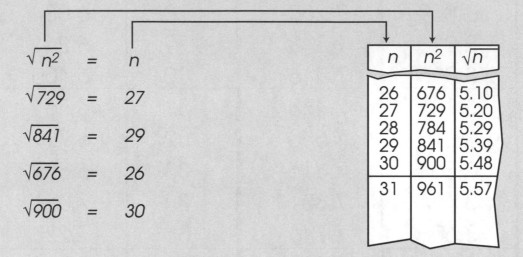

$$\sqrt{n^2} = n$$

$$\sqrt{729} = 27$$

$$\sqrt{841} = 29$$

$$\sqrt{676} = 26$$

$$\sqrt{900} = 30$$

n	n²	√n
26	676	5.10
27	729	5.20
28	784	5.29
29	841	5.39
30	900	5.48
31	961	5.57

The Pythagorean Theorem

In a right triangle, the square of the length of the hypotenuse (the longest side) is equal to the sum of the squares of the lengths of the legs (the shorter sides).

In the diagram at the left, $a = 3$, $b = 4$, $c = 5$.

$$a^2 + b^2 = c^2$$

$$3^2 + 4^2 = 5^2$$

$$9 + 16 = 25$$

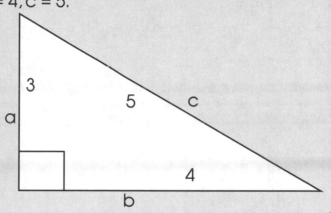

The Pythagorean Theorem states that the square of the hypotenuse is equal to the sum of the squares of the legs. Use the formula $a^2 + b^2 = c^2$, where a and b are the legs and c is the hypotenuse.

$$x^2 + 9^2 = 15^2$$

$$x^2 + 81 = 225$$

$$x^2 = 225 - 81$$

$$x^2 = 144$$

$$x^2 = \sqrt{144} \quad \text{so } x = 12$$

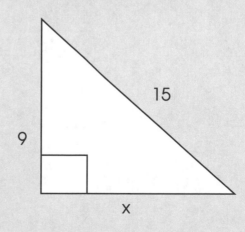

The Pythagorean Theorem

Study how the Pythagorean Theorem and the ratios of similar triangles are used to find the measures of $\overline{AB}$, the measures of $\overline{A'C'}$, and the measure of $\overline{B'C'}$

right $\triangle ABC \sim$ right $A'B'C'$

Step 1

Use $c^2 = a^2 + b^2$ to find the measure of $\overline{AB}$.

$c^2 = a^2 + b^2$

$c^2 = 6^2 + 8^2$

$c^2 = 100$

$c = 10$

$AB = 10$

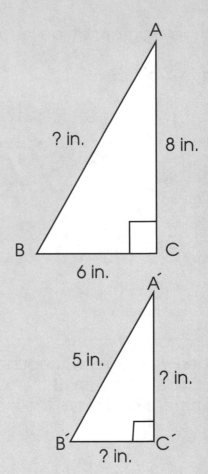

Step 2

Use the measure of $\overline{AB}$ from Step 1 and find the measure of $\overline{A'C'}$ and $\overline{B'C'}$.

$$\frac{AB}{A'B'} = \frac{AC}{A'C'} \qquad\qquad \frac{AB}{A'B'} = \frac{BC}{B'C'}$$

$$\frac{10}{5} = \frac{8}{A'C'} \qquad\qquad \frac{10}{5} = \frac{6}{B'C'}$$

$\overline{AB}$ is 10 inches long.

$\overline{A'C'}$ is 4 inches long.

$$A'C' = 4 \qquad\qquad B'C' = 3$$

$\overline{B'C'}$ is 3 inches long.

Perimeter

The **perimeter** is the distance around a shape.

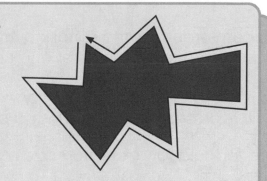

Examples:

Find the perimeter of a polygon by adding the lengths of each side.

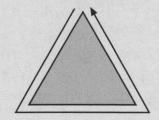

5 cm   5 cm

6 cm

5 + 5 + 6 = 16 cm

3 in.

3 in.   3 in.

3 in.

3 + 3 + 3 + 3 = 12 in.

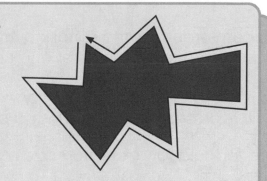

3 + 4 + 2 + 3 + 3 + 4 + 2 + 2 +
3 + 3 + 2 + 4 + 2 + 3 + 3 = 43 cm

The perimeter of some polygons can be given as a formula.

Examples:

The sides of a square are the same length.
The perimeter equals 4 times the length of a side (s).

Perimeter of a square: s + s + s + s = 4 x s = 4s

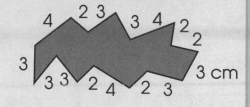

s = side

The opposite sides of a rectangle
are the same length. The perimeter equals
2 times the length (l) plus 2 times the width (w).

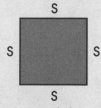

w = width

l = length

Perimeter of a rectangle: 2l + 2w

Circumference, Diameter, and Radius of a Circle

Circumference is the distance around a circle. The **diameter** is a line segment that passes through the center of a circle and has both end points on the circle.

To find the circumference of any circle, multiply 3.14 times the diameter. The number 3.14 represents **pi** (pronounced *pie*) and is often written by this Greek symbol, π.

The formula for circumference is C = π x d

    C = circumference

    d = diameter

    π = 3.14

Example:

    Circle A
    d = 2 in.
    C = 3.14 x 2 in.
    C = 6.28 in.

The **radius** of a circle is the distance from the center of the circle to its outside edge. The diameter equals two times the radius.

Find the circumference by multiplying π (3.14) times the diameter or by multiplying π (3.14) times 2r (2 times the radius).

C = π x d or C = π x 2r

Area of a Rectangle and a Square

Example:

The **area** of a shape is the amount of space it covers. Area is measured in square units, such as square centimeters (cm^2) or square inches (in^2).

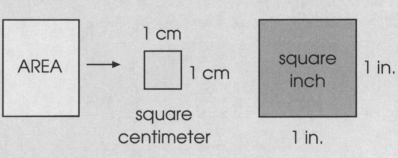

AREA → square centimeter (1 cm × 1 cm)

square inch (1 in. × 1 in.)

One way to measure the area of a shape is to count the number of square units it covers.

1	2	3	4	5	6
7	8	9	10	11	12
13	14	15	16	17	18

The area of this rectangle is 18 square units.

To find the **area** of a square or rectangle, multiply the length by the width.

Example:

2 in.

3 in.

Area = 2 in. x 3 in.
= 6 square in.
= 6 in.^{2}

Area of a square = side x side = s x s = s^2

Area of a rectangle = length x width = l x w = lw

s

w

l

Area of a triangle = $\frac{1}{2}$ base x height = $\frac{1}{2}$bh

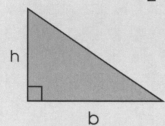 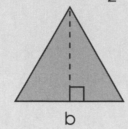 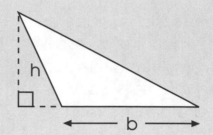

To find the area of a parallelogram, split it into two identical triangles.

 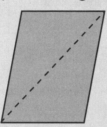  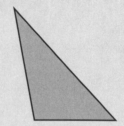

Area of a parallelogram = base x height = bh

h = height

b = base

The ancient Greeks discovered that the area of a circle is related to the radius by π.

Example:

Area of a circle = π x radius x radius = πr^2

Find the area of this circle.

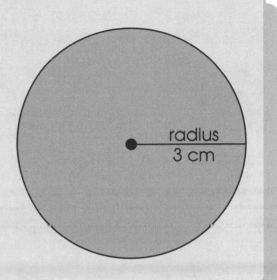

radius
3 cm

$A = (\pi) \times (3 \text{ cm}) \times (3 \text{ cm})$
$\quad = 9\pi$
$\quad = 9 \times 3.14$
$\quad \approx 28.26 \text{ cm}^2$

Shapes created by combining 2 or more polygons are called **compound figures**. To find the area of a compound figure, divide it into shapes with known areas such as triangles, circles, and squares. Then, find the area of each shape and add or subtract.

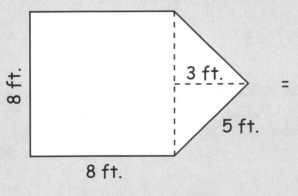

8 ft.

3 ft.

5 ft.

8 ft.

$A = 64 \text{ ft.}^2 + 12 \text{ ft.}^2$
$\quad = 76 \text{ ft.}^2$

=

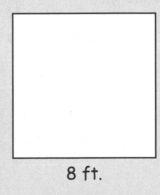

8 ft.

$A = 8 \text{ ft.} \times 8 \text{ ft.}$
$\quad = 64 \text{ ft.}^2$

+

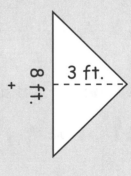

8 ft.

3 ft.

$A = \quad (8 \times 3)$
$\quad = 12 \text{ ft.}^2$

Space Figures

Space figures are figures whose points are in more than one plane. Cubes and cylinders are space figures.

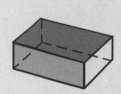 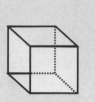 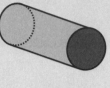

rectangular prism   **cone**   **cube**   **cylinder**   **sphere**   **pyramid**

A **prism** has two identical, parallel bases.

All of the faces on a **rectangular prism** are rectangles.

A **cube** is a prism with six identical, square faces.

A **pyramid** is a space figure whose base is a polygon and whose faces are triangles with a common vertex—the point where two rays meet.

A **cylinder** has a curved surface and two parallel bases that are identical circles.

A **cone** has one circular, flat face and one vertex.

A **sphere** has no flat surface. All points are an equal distance from the center.

Volume of a Box

The **volume** of a 3-D shape is the amount of space it occupies. Volume is measured in cubic units, such as cubic centimeters (cm^3) or cubic inches (in.^{3}).

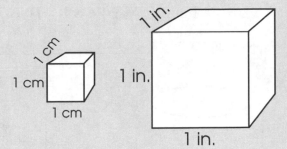

Imagine a box filled with unit cubes. The number of cubes is the volume of the box.

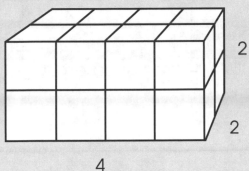

The formula for finding the volume of a box is length times width times height **(L x W x H)**. The answer is given in cubic units.

The box has a volume of 16 cubic units.

Volume of a Cylinder, a Pyramid, and a Sphere

To find the volume of a **cylinder**, a **pyramid**, and a **sphere**, follow these directions:

volume of a cylinder	volume of a pyramid	volume of a sphere

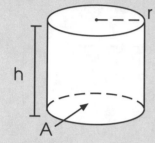
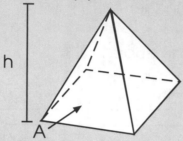

V = area of base x height
$= \pi r^2 h$

V = area of base x height x $\frac{1}{3}$
$= \frac{1}{3} Ah$

$V = \frac{4}{3}\pi r^3$

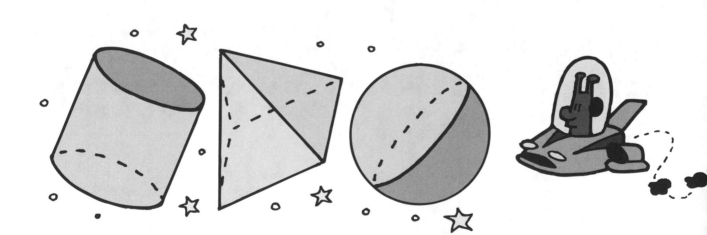

ORGANIZING
AND
GRAPHING DATA

Rob is training for the javelin throw at a big track meet. He wants to know how he is doing, so he records the distances of 10 throws he makes during practice. What is Rob's average distance?

Throw	Distance	Throw	Distance
1	23 feet	6	20 feet
2	26 feet	7	24 feet
3	21 feet	8	23 feet
4	23 feet	9	22 feet
5	25 feet	10	22 feet

The average of a group of numbers tells something about the main trend of the data. The three most important kinds of averages are called the **mode**, the **median**, and the **mean**. The **range** is the difference between the highest and lowest number in a group of numbers.

Mode

The **mode** is the number in the data that occurs most often. The mode of the javelin distances is 23 feet, since that number appears three times—more often than any other does. If the data do not have a number that appears more than once, there is no mode. For example, the numbers 6, 4, 8, 7, 5, 3, and 9 have no mode.

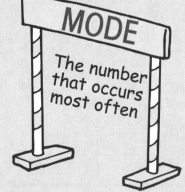

MODE

The number that occurs most often

A group of numbers can also have more than one mode. For example, the numbers 2, 5, 4, 3, 2, 3, and 6 have two modes since 2 and 3 both occur twice.

If a group of numbers does have a mode, the mode will always be one of the numbers in the list.

Median

The **median** is another kind of average.
When ordering a list of numbers from least to greatest, the median is the number that falls in the middle. Look at Anna's maximum high jumps for the last week.

Day	Height
Monday	62 inches
Tuesday	64 inches
Wednesday	62 inches
Thursday	64 inches
Friday	60 inches
Saturday	61 inches
Sunday	64 inches

Order the numbers: 60, 61, 62, **62**, 64, 64, 64. The number 62 falls in the middle. It is the median.

The mode is 64 inches. In some cases, the median and mode are the same number.

If there is an even number of heights, there will be two numbers in the middle. To find the median, add the two middle numbers and divide the sum by 2.

MEDIAN

The middle number in an ordered list of numbers

Example: 2, 2, 3, 4, 6, 6, 7, 9

The numbers 4 and 6 are both in the middle.
4 + 6 = 10; 10 ÷ 2 = 5. The median is 5. The median does not have to be a number in the list.

Mean

Probably the most common average is the **mean**. To find the mean, add all the numbers in the list, then divide the sum by the total number of addends.

Suppose a hurdler completes his trials in the following times. Find the mean.

Trial	Time in Seconds
1	35
2	29
3	34
4	30
5	31
6	33

MEAN

The sum of all the numbers divided by the number of addends

Add the numbers: 35 + 29 + 34 + 30 + 31 + 33 = 192
Divide 192 by 6 because there are 6 numbers in the list: 192 ÷ 6 = 32.
The mean is 32 seconds.

The mean may or may not be a number in the list. The mean may also be different from the median and/or the mode.

Tables and Bar Graphs

Tables

Organizing data into **tables** makes it easier to compare numbers. As evident in the example, putting many numbers in a paragraph is confusing. When the same numbers are organized in a table, you can compare numbers in a glance. Tables can be arranged several ways and still be easy to read and understand.

Example: Money spent on groceries:
Family A: week 1 — $68.50; week 2 — $72.25; week 3 — $67.00; week 4 — $74.50.
Family B: week 1 — $42.25; week 2 — $47.50; week 3 — $50.25; week 4 — $53.50.

	Week 1	Week 2	Week 3	Week 4
Family A	$68.50	$72.25	$67.00	$74.50
Family B	$42.25	$47.50	$50.25	$53.50

Bar Graphs

Another way to organize information is a **bar graph**. The bar graph in the example compares the number of students in 4 elementary schools. Each bar stands for 1 school. You can easily see that School A has the most students and School C has the least. The numbers along the left show how many students attend each school.

Example:

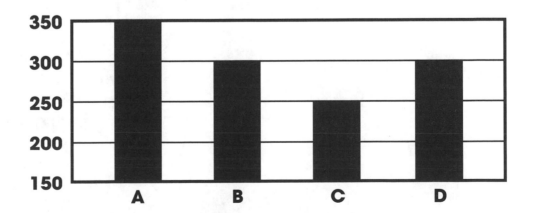

Picture Graphs and Circle Graphs

The Picture Graph

Newspapers and textbooks often use pictures in graphs instead of bars. Each picture stands for a certain number of objects. Half a picture means half the number. The **picture graph** in the example indicates the number of games each team won. The Astros won 7 games, so they have $3\frac{1}{2}$ balls.

Example:

	Games Won			
Astros	⚾	⚾	⚾	◖
Orioles	⚾	⚾		
Bluebirds	⚾	⚾	⚾	⚾
Sluggers	⚾			

(1 ball = 2 games)

The Circle Graph

Circle graphs are useful in showing how something is divided into parts. The circle graph in the example shows how Carly spent her $10 allowance. Each section is a fraction of her whole allowance. For example, the movie tickets section is $\frac{1}{2}$ of the circle, showing that she spent $\frac{1}{2}$ of her allowance, $5, on movie tickets.

Example:

Line Graphs and Multiple Line Graphs

Line Graph

Average Rainfall in Valdivia, Chile

Line graphs make it easy to see change.

June has the most rainfall, about 17.5 inches.

The scale cannot be read exactly, so you must **estimate** each amount.

In what month does Valdivia get the least rainfall?   January

What is the average rainfall for August in Valdivia?   13 inches

Multiple Line Graph

Multiple line graphs make it easy to see change and to compare numbers. Notice that a different kind of line is used for each type of item sold. The **key** shows what each line represents.

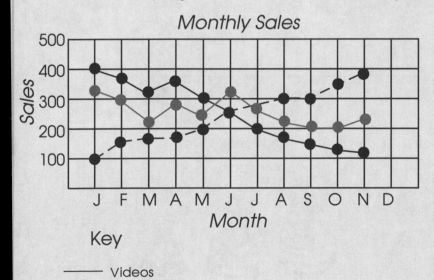

Monthly Sales

Key

—— Videos

—— CDs

– – Cassettes

Item	December Sales
Videos	180
CDs	450
Cassettes	360

Integers

An **integer** is any positive or negative whole number, or zero. Negative integers are numbers less than zero. The opposite of any number is found the same distance from 0 on a number line.

Example:

35 below zero can be written as −35.
The opposite of 6 is −6.
The opposite of −41 is 41.
The opposite of 0 is 0.

Example:

When ordering integers, compare two numbers at a time. A number line can help.

Put the numbers −4, 2, 0 in order from greatest to least.
−4 is less than 2.
2 is greater than 0.
0 is greater than −4.
2, 0, −4 shows the numbers in order from greatest to least.

Adding Integers

Example:

A **number line** can be used to add intergers. To add positive integers, move to the right. To add negative integers, move to the left.

$4 + (-5) = (-1)$
Find 4 on the number line. Move 5 spaces to the left.

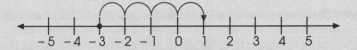

$(-3) + 4 = 1$

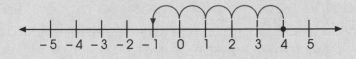

$(-2) + (-1) = (-3)$

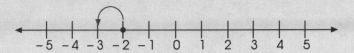

Subtracting Integers

Example:

Steps:

To subtract integers, change the subtraction problem to an addition problem. Then, change the second number in the problem to its opposite. (A −2 will be a 2; a 2 will be a −2.) Use a number line to solve the problem.

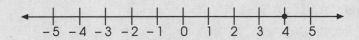

$2 - 4 = 2 + (-4) = -2$ $3 - (-1) = 3 + 1 = 4$ $(-3) - 1 = (-3) + (-1) = -4$

$(-1) - (-3) = (-1) + 3 = 2$ $(-4) - (-4) = (-4) + 4 = 0$

Multiplying Integers

Multiplying Integers

Example:

Ignore the negative signs, and multiply the numbers. If two factors have the same sign, the product is positive. If two factors have different signs, the product is negative. With three or more factors, multiply two numbers at a time and keep track of the signs.

$2 \times 3 = 6$ $2 \times -3 = -6$ $-2 \times 3 = -6$ $-2 \times -3 = 6$

$2 \times 3 \times -2 = 6 \times -2 = -12$ $2 \times -3 \times -2 = -6 \times -2 = 12$

$-2 \times -3 \times -2 = 6 \times -2 = -12$

Properties of Multiplication

Example:

Property	Definition	Example
Zero	Any number times 0 equals 0.	$4 \times 0 = 0$
Identity	Any number times 1 equals the number.	$4 \times 1 = 4$
Commutative	The order of the factors does not change the product.	$2 \times 3 = 3 \times 2$
Associative	The grouping of the factors does not change the product.	$(2 \times 3) \times 4 = 2 \times (3 \times 4)$

Dividing Integers

Dividing Integers

Example:

The rules for dividing integers are the same for multiplying integers.

1. Ignore the signs, and divide the numbers.
2. If the dividend and divisor have the same sign, the product is positive.
3. If the dividend and divisor have different signs, the product is negative.

$15 \div 3 = 5$
$-15 \div 3 = -5$
$15 \div -3 = -5$
$-15 \div -3 = 5$

My Dear Aunt Sally

Example:

To solve a problem with several operations, follow the rules of My Dear Aunt Sally.

My Dear =   **M**ultiplication/**D**ivision

Aunt Sally =   **A**ddition/**S**ubtraction

Do all multiplication and division steps first, in order from left to right. Then do all addition and subtraction steps, in order from left to right.

These rules are called the **Order of Operations**.

$4 \times 8 + 36 \div 6 - 7$

$32 \quad + \quad 6 \; - \; 7$

$38 \; - \; 7$

31

X and Y Coordinates

A graph with horizontal and vertical number lines can show the location of certain points. The horizontal number line is called the **x axis**, and the vertical number line is called the **y axis**. Two numbers, called the **x coordinate** and the **y coordinate**, show where a point is on the graph.

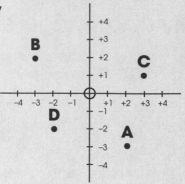

The first coordinate, x, tells how many units to the right or left of 0 the point is located. On the example graph, point A is +2, two units to the right of 0.

The second coordinate, y, tells how many units above or below 0 the point is located. On the example, point A is –3, three units below 0.

Thus, the coordinates of A are +2, –3. The coordinates of B are –3, +2. (Notice the order of the coordinates.) The coordinates of C are +3, +1; and D, –2, –2.

Ordered pairs is another term used to describe pairs of integers used to locate points on a graph.

Plotting points on a **scatter plot** can help determine whether the data values indicate a trend.

Case 1: An **increase** in one value results in an **increase** in the other ⟶ **positive correlation**

case 2: An **increase** in one value results in a **decrease** in the other ⟶ **negative correlation**

Case 3: Neither Case 1 nor Case 2 ⟶ **no correlation**

Examples:

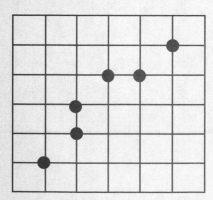

Positive correlation

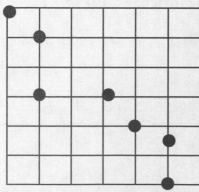

Negative correlation

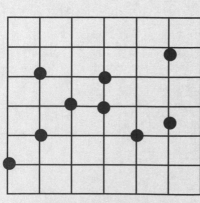

No correlation

Venn Diagram

A **Venn diagram** (named for English mathematician John Venn) is a graphic way of showing how two or more groups of information overlap or have shared features. Each circle represents one of the sets, or groups, of information. The overlapping section shows the shared features.

This Venn diagram shows the factors and common factors for 48 and 80.

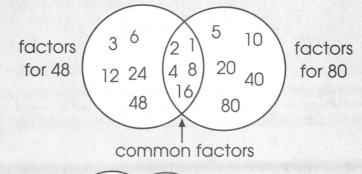

factors for 48

3 6
12 24
48

2 1
4 8
16

5 10
20
40
80

factors for 80

common factors

This Venn diagram shows the results of a reading survey.

number of people who read book 1 only

8 | 3 | 6

number of people who read book 2 only

number of people who read both books

Glossary

Abacus: The world's oldest counting machine, which originated in China.

Acute angle: An angle that measures less than 90°.

Acute triangle: A triangle in which all angles measure less than 90°.

Adjacent angles: Angles that share a vertex and a ray.

Angle: What is formed when two line segments come together.

Area: The amount of space a shape covers, measured in square units. The formula for a square or rectangle is length x width. The formula for a triangle is $\frac{1}{2}$ base x height. The formula for a parallelogram is base x height.

Associative property: The grouping of the factors does not change the product.

Bar graphs: A way of organizing information, in which the height or length of the bars (depending on the orientation of the bars) show how much. The higher or longer the bar, the more there is of something.

Capacity: The measure of how much liquid a container will hold.

Celsius: The metric unit of temperature. Water freezes at 0° C and boils at 100° C.

Center: The point from which all points on a circle are the same distance.

Centi- (c): $\frac{1}{100}$ as a fraction and 0.01 as a decimal.

Centimeter (cm): $\frac{1}{100}$ of a meter or 0.4 inches.

Chord: A line segment that connects two points on a circle but does not pass through the center point.

Circle: A shape on which all of the points on it are the same distance from a given point.

Circle graph: A kind of graph that is useful for showing how something is divided into parts.

Circumference: The distance around a circle.

Common factors: Factors that are the same.

Common multiples: Multiples that two or more numbers share, or have in common. Multiples of 8: 8, 16, 24, 32, 40, 48, 56, 64, 72, 80....Multiples of 12: 12, 24, 36, 48, 60, 72, 84....Common multiples of 8 and 12 are 24, 48, and 72.

Commutative property: The order of the factors does not change the product.

Complementary angles: Angles that combine to make a 90° angle.

Composite number: Any number that is not a prime number. That is, it can be divided evenly by numbers other than itself and 1. The first 10 composite numbers are 4, 6, 8, 9, 10, 12, 14, 15, 16, and 18.

Glossary

Compound figures: Shapes created by combining 2 or more polygons.

Compound interest: Interest paid on the original principal and the interest already earned.

Cone: A 3-dimensional figure with one circular, flat face and one vertex.

Congruent shape: Shapes that are exactly the same size and shape.

Cube: A prism with six identical, square faces.

Cup: A customary unit of capacity. 1 cup = 8 ounces

Customary System: Measures length in inches and feet, capacity in cups and pints, weight in ounces and pounds, and temperature in Fahrenheit.

Cylinder: A 3-dimensional figure with a curved surface and two parallel bases that are identical circles.

Deci- (d): Represents $\frac{1}{10}$.

Decimal: A number that includes a period called a decimal point. The digits to the right of the decimal point are a value less than one.

Deka- (da): Represents 10.

Denominator: The bottom number in a fraction.

Diameter: A line segment that passes through the center of a circle and has both end points on the circle.

Dividend: The number to be divided in a division problem.

Divisor: The number used to divide another number.

Egyptian numeral system: An early numbering system based on the number 10.

Equation: A number sentence in which the value on the left of the equal sign must equal the value on the right of the equal sign.

Equilateral triangle: A triangle with three equal sides.

Estimating: Using an approximate number instead of an exact one.

Expanded notation: Writing out the value of each digit in a number.

Factor: A number that can be multiplied by another number to give a certain product. The factors of 24 are 1, 2, 3, 4, 6, 8, 12, and 24 because 1 x 24 = 24, 2 x 12 = 24, 3 x 8 = 24, and 4 x 6 = 24.

Fahrenheit: The customary unit of temperature measured in degrees.

Glossary

Fluid ounce: A customary unit of liquid measurement.

Foot: A customary unit for measuring length. 3 feet = 1 yard

Fraction: A number that names part of something.

Gallon: A customary unit of capacity. 1 gallon = 4 quarts

Geometry: The branch of mathematics that has to do with points, lines, and shapes.

Gram (g): The basic metric unit of weight. A gram is about 0.035 oz.

Greatest common factor (GCF): The largest number that will divide evenly into a set of number

Hecto- (h): Represents 100 units.

Horizontal line segment: A line with two endpoints that extends horizontally.

Improper fraction: A fraction that has a larger numerator than its denominator.

Inch: The smallest customary unit of length. Twelve inches = 1 foot

Integer: Any positive or negative whole number, or zero.

Interest: The money paid for the use of money.

Intersecting lines: Lines that meet at a point.

Isosceles triangle: A triangle with two equal sides.

Key: In a graph, this shows what each line represents.

Kilo- (k): Represents 1,000 units.

Kilogram (kg): 1,000 g or about 2.2 lb.

Kiloliter (kL): 1,000 liters or about 250 gallons.

Kilometer (km): 1,000 meters or 0.6 miles.

Least common multiple (LCM): The lowest possible multiple any pair of numbers have in commo

Line: A line that extends forever in both directions.

Line graph: This kind of graph makes it easy to see change when comparing something; for instance, rainfall for the year, month by month.

Line of symmetry: A line that divides a shape into two matching halves. A shape can have an number of lines of symmetry.

Line segment: A line that has two endpoints.

Glossary

Liter (L): The basic metric unit of capacity. It is a little more than 1 quart.

Mean: The most common average; to find the mean, add all the numbers in the list, then divide the sum by the total number of addends.

Median: A kind of average; when ordering a list of numbers from least to greatest, it is the number that falls in the middle.

Mental math: The kind of math you can do in your head, without paper.

Meter (m): The basic metric unit of length, which is about 40 inches or 3.3 feet.

Metric system: Measures length in meters, capacity in liters, mass in grams, and temperature in Celsius.

Metric ton (t): 1,000 kg or about 1.1 tn.

Mile: A customary measurement of length. 5,280 feet or 1,760 yards = 1 mile.

Milli- (m): $\frac{1}{1000}$ as a fraction and 0.001 as a decimal.

Milliliter (mL): $\frac{1}{1000}$ of a liter or about 0.03 oz.

Milligram (mg): $\frac{1}{1000}$ g or about 0.000035 oz.

Millimeter (mm): $\frac{1}{1000}$ of a meter or 0.04 inches.

Mixed number: A whole number and a fraction, such as $1\frac{1}{2}$.

Mode: A kind of average; it is the number in the data that occurs most often.

Multiple: The product of any given number and a factor such as 1, 2, 3, and so on.

Multiple line graph: Used to make it easy to see change and to compare numbers. For instance, if you want to show sales of videos, CDs, and cassettes month-by-month, you would use this type of graph.

My Dear Aunt Sally: To solve a problem with several operations, follow the rules of My Dear Aunt Sally. Do all multiplication and division steps first, in order from left to right. Then do all addition and subtraction steps, in order from left to right.

Negative correlation: In a scatter plot, an increase in one value results in an decrease in the other.

Numerator: The top number in a fraction.

Number line: A line that can be used to add integers. To add positive integers, move to the right. To add negative integers, move to the left.

Obtuse angle: An angle that measures more than 90°.

Obtuse triangle: A triangle in which one angle measure more than 90°.

Glossary

Order of operations: The name of the rules that describe the order in which you solve a problem; all multiplication and division steps are performed first, in order from left to right. All addition and subtraction steps are performed next, in order from left to right.

Ordered pairs: Two integers used to locate points on a graph.

Ordering integers: Comparing two numbers at a time.

Ounce: The smallest unit of weight in the customary system. 16 ounces = 1 pound

Outcome: Each possible result in a probability experiment.

Parallel lines: Lines that are in the same plane and never intersect.

Parallelogram: A quadrilateral with four parallel sides, with the opposite sides of equal length, but all its angles are more than or less than 90°.

Percent: A kind of ratio that compares a number to 100. "Percent" means "for each hundred."

Perimeter: The distance around a shape formed by straight lines. The perimeter of a square is 4 x s = 4s. The perimeter of a rectangle is 2l + 2w.

Perpendicular lines: Lines that intersect and form a right angle.

Pi: The number 3.14, which is the number you use to multiply times the diameter to find the circumference of any circle.

Picture graphs: Similar to a bar graph, the picture graph uses a picture to represent a certain amount. For instance, you might use 1 ball to show every 2 games won.

Pint: A customary unit of capacity. 1 pint = 2 cups

Place value: The position of a digit in a number which shows its value.

Polygon: A shape that means "many angles" and has 3 properties: 1) starts and stops at the same place (making it "closed"); 2) can be traced without lifting the pencil or crossing or retracing any part; 3) is made of at least three line segments.

Positive correlation: In a scatter plot, an increase in one value results in an increase in the other.

Pound: A customary unit of weight. 16 ounces = 1 pound

Prime number: Any number greater than 1 that can only be divided evenly by itself and the number 1. The first 10 prime numbers are 2, 3, 5, 7, 11, 13, 17, 19, 23, and 29.

Principal: The amount of money borrowed or deposited.

Prism: A 3-dimensional shape with two identical, parallel bases.

Probability: The ratio of favorable outcomes to possible outcomes in an experiment.

Product: The quantity that results from multiplying two or more numbers.

Glossary

Proportion: A statement that two ratios are equal.

Pyramid: A space figure whose base is a polygon and whose faces are triangles with a common vertex—the point where two rays meet.

Pythagorean theorem: A formula that states that the square of the hypotenuse is equal to the sum of the squares of the legs, or $a^2 + b^2 = c^2$.

Quadrilateral: A shape with four sides and four angles, with a total sum of angles being 360°.

Quart: A customary unit of capacity. 1 quart = 2 pints

Quotient: The answer in a division problem.

Radius: The distance from the center of the circle to its outside edge.

Range: The difference between the highest and lowest number in a group of numbers.

Rate of interest: The amount of interest, usually expressed as a percent.

Ratio: A comparison of two quantities.

Ray: A line that extends in one direction forever.

Rectangle: A quadrilateral with four parallel sides, but only its opposite sides are equal length. It has four 90° angles.

Reflexive property: $a = a$. Example: 3 = 3

Regular polygon: A polygon that has sides that are all the same length.

Right angle: An angle that measures 90°.

Right triangle: A triangle in which one angle measures 90°.

Roman numerals: An early numbering system based on 10 and represented with letters, which is still in use today.

Rounding: Expressing a number to the nearest ten, hundred, thousand, and so on.

Sample space: A list or table of all the possible outcomes of an experiment.

Scalene triangle: A triangle with no equal sides.

Scatter plot: Where points are plotted to help determine whether the data values indicate a trend.

Similar shape: Shapes that are about the same relative size.

Space figures: Figures whose points are in more than one plane; for example, cubes and cylinders.

Sphere: A 3-dimensional shape with no flat surface. All points are an equal distance from the center.

Glossary

Square: A quadrilateral with four parallel sides of equal length and four 90° angles.

Square root: The number multiplied by itself. For instance, 2^2 means 2 x 2, which equals 4.

Standardized units: Units agreed upon all over the world so that measurement made in India are the same as measurements made in Iceland.

Straight angle: An angle that equals exactly 180°.

Supplementary angles: Angles that combine to make a 180° angle.

Symmetric: A geometric shape that can be separated into two identical parts.

Symmetric property: If a = b, then b = a. Example: If 6 = 2x, then 2x = 6.

Tables: Organizing data in a format that it makes it easier to compare numbers.

Time (interest): The period of time for which money is borrowed, usually expressed in years.

Ton: A customary unit of weight. 2,000 lbs. = 1 ton

Transformations: Changing shapes by sliding, flipping, and rotating them.

Transitive property: If a = b and b = c, then a = c. Example: If y = 3x, and 3x = 12, then y = 12.

Trapezoid: A quadrilateral with two opposite sides that are parallel; its sides may or may not be equal length; its angles may include none, one, or two that are 90°.

Trial and error: A problem-solving strategy in which a guess is made at the answer to see if it works.

Triangle: A three-sided polygon, with three sides and three angles.

Venn diagram: A graphic way of showing how two or more groups of information overlap or have shared features. Each circle represents one of the sets, or groups, of information. The overlapping section shows the shared features.

Vertical angles: Angles that are not adjacent, but they share a vertex and are congruent.

Vertical line segment: A line that extends vertically and has two endpoints.

Volume: The number of cubic units that fills a space.

Weight: The measure of the force of gravity applied to an object.

X axis: The horizontal number line in a plotting graph.

X/Y coordinate: Show where a point is on a plotting graph.

Y axis: The vertical number line in a plotting graph.

Yard: A customary unit for measuring length. 1,760 yards = 1mile